The Story of Anna Kingsford and Edward Maitland and of the new Gospel of Interpretation

Samuel Hopgood Hart

Alpha Editions

This edition published in 2024

ISBN : 9789362928047

Design and Setting By
Alpha Editions
www.alphaedis.com
Email - info@alphaedis.com

As per information held with us this book is in Public Domain.
This book is a reproduction of an important historical work. Alpha Editions uses the best technology to reproduce historical work in the same manner it was first published to preserve its original nature. Any marks or number seen are left intentionally to preserve its true form.

Contents

PREFACE TO THE THIRD EDITION. ....- 1 -

INTRODUCTION. 5

CHAPTER I. THE VOCATION. 8

CHAPTER II. THE INITIATION. 28

CHAPTER III. THE COMMUNICATION. 47

CHAPTER IV. THE ANTAGONISATION. 71

CHAPTER V. THE RECAPITULATION. 91

CHAPTER VI. THE EXEMPLIFICATION. 103

CHAPTER VII. THE PROMULGATION
AND RECOGNITION.. 119

PREFACE
TO THE THIRD EDITION.

Since the publication in 1893 of this book which, as stated in Chapter VII., was "intended but as an epitome and instalment" of a far larger book then in course of preparation, the full and final account of the "New Gospel of Interpretation" has been given to the world. In 1896 Edward Maitland published his *magnum opus*, "The Life of Anna Kingsford," in two large volumes of 420 pages, "illustrated with portraits, views, and facsimiles." This is, and will always be, the biography *par excellence* of Anna Kingsford and Edward Maitland, and it is absolutely indispensable for those who would know all that there is to be known of them and their work and of the "New Gospel of Interpretation." As that book, however, on account of its great length, must always be a costly book, and therefore beyond the means of many who would like to have some reliable information concerning Anna Kingsford and Edward Maitland and their work, and as there are many who, on account of their time for reading being limited or their inclination to read being little, require information within the compass of a small book or go without it altogether, there will, notwithstanding the publication of the "Life of Anna Kingsford," be a demand for this shorter "Story," which is so admirably suited to meet the needs or requirements of these classes of persons; for, be it noted, the publication of "The Life of Anna Kingsford" has not in any way depreciated the value of this book in this sense that, having been written by one of the two recipients of the "New Gospel of Interpretation," it is a first authority second to none for the statements therein contained.

The change in the title of the book from "The Story of the New Gospel of Interpretation" to the present title calls for some explanation and justification, because the former title was an excellent one in many respects, and the book has become known to many by that title. The "Gospel of Interpretation" is the name or description which was given by its Divine Inspirers, the Hierarchy of the Spheres Celestial, to the work of which this book tells the story, in token of its relation to the previous "Gospel of Manifestation." The former title implied, as the Author pointed out in his preface, that that which this book propounded was "not really a new Gospel, but one of Interpretation only"; and this is not really new, but, as the Author has also pointed out, "so old as to have become forgotten and lost, being the purely spiritual sense, as discerned from the purely spiritual standpoint originally intended and insisted on by Scripture itself as its true sense and standpoint, and those which alone render Scripture intelligible"[1]. But notwithstanding this, and notwithstanding that on the front page it was expressly stated that "There shall nothing new be told; but that which is ancient shall be interpreted," the former title failed to convey to the minds of some the meaning that it was intended to convey, and it gave no indication of the biographical nature of the work. Many who otherwise would have read the book refrained from doing so because they thought that a new Gospel, inconsistent with and perhaps opposed to if not intended to supersede the old Gospel, was propounded. It is necessary, therefore, for me to state, if possible more explicitly than it was stated in the previous editions of this book, that this is not an attempt to create a new Gospel differing from that of Jesus Christ[2]. Anna Kingsford's and Edward Maitland's mission and aim was to interpret the Christ, not to rival or supersede Him. The "New Gospel" is, first and foremost, *interpretative*, and is destructive only in the sense of reconstructive. "It tells nothing new; it simply restores and reinforces the old, even the Gnosis, which, as the doctrine of the Church unfallen, is that also of the Church fallen, though the latter has lost the key to its interpretation"[3]. Nor is the teaching represented by this book opposed to the existence of an objective Church. Anna Kingsford and Edward Maitland fully recognised the necessity of such an organisation for the formulation, propagation, and exposition of religion. Their opposition was "only to the recognition by the Church of the objective, historical, and materialistic aspect of religion, *to the exclusion* of that which really constitutes religion, namely, its subjective, spiritual, and substantial aspect, wherein alone it appeals to the mind and soul, and is efficacious for redemption." The aim of the New Gospel "is defined exactly," said Edward Maitland, "in the following citation from St. Dionysius the Areopagite 'not to destroy, but to construct; or, rather, to destroy by construction; to conquer error by the full presentment of truth.' As will be obvious, such a design does not necessarily involve the destruction of anything that exists whether of symbol or ritual, or ecclesiastical organisation, but only their regeneration by means of their translation into their spiritual and divinely intended sense. And it is precisely because that sense has been lost—as declared in Scripture it had long been, and would yet long be, lost—that a new 'Gospel of Interpretation' has been vouchsafed in fulfilment of the promises in Scripture to that effect; and this from the source of the original Divine revelation, namely, the Church Celestial, and by the method which always was that of such revelation, namely, the intuition operating under special illumination.... Even the priest, though hitherto deservedly regarded as the 'enemy of man,' will not be destroyed under the new *régime* whose inauguration we are witnessing. For in becoming interpreter as well as administrator, he will be prophet as well as priest, and speak out the things of God and the soul instead of concealing them under a veil. So will the 'veil be taken away,' and Cain, the priest, instead of killing Abel, the prophet, as hitherto, will unite with him, becoming prophet and priest in one. And instead of any longer corrupting the 'woman' Intuition, and suppressing the 'man' Intellect, he will purify and exalt her, and enable her to fulfil her proper function as 'the Mother of God' in man, and will recognise the intellect, when duly conjoined with her, as the heir of all things. Thus, becoming interpreter as well as administrator, prophet as well as priest, and recognising interpretation as the corollary of the understanding, the prophet-priest of the regeneration will give to men freely of the waters of life, that only true bread of Heaven, which is the food of the understanding, instead of the indigestible 'stones' and poisonous 'serpents' of doctrines, the profession of which, by divorcing assent from conviction, involves that moral and intellectual suicide, to induce others to join him in committing which Cardinal Newman wrote his 'Grammar of Assent,' True it is 'faith that saves,' but the faith that is without understanding is not faith, but credulity"[4]. It is for the above-mentioned reasons that the title of this book has been changed. The title must be subservient to the book, and it is hoped that, the change having been made, there will not be any further misunderstanding—even on the part of those who are most superficial—as to the nature and object of "The Story of the New Gospel of Interpretation."

Edward Maitland did not long survive the completion of the great task that he undertook when he set himself to write a full account of his life and that of his colleague. He retained his full mental vigour until the publication of "The Life of Anna Kingsford"; but after that he rapidly declined, and on the 2nd October, 1897, at the close of his seventy-third year, a little over nine years after the death of Anna Kingsford[5], he passed away peacefully at "The Warders" at Tonbridge, the home (at that time) of his friends Colonel and Mrs. Currie, with whom, and under whose loving care, he spent the last few months of his life—a life concerning which, as also that of Anna Kingsford, I will not say anything here, for this book will testify. Blessed are the souls whom the just commemorate before God.

Many who read these pages will not rest until they know more of those great prophets the story of whose lives is here told, and of the Divine Gnosis that it was their high mission to proclaim. I have indicated whence they can obtain this information. This "Story," interesting as it is and much as there is in it, is little more than an indication of some of the facts that are fully stated and dealt with in "The Life of Anna Kingsford," and there is much of importance that (as it could not possibly receive proper treatment in a book of this size) was passed over here to be related in the larger biography. I have not thought it expedient to alter the character of or to add much to this book, but I have enlarged it by incorporating therein, from "The Life of Anna Kingsford," some additional matter which is of interest, and which should add to the value of the book. The most important additions are the account of Anna Kingsford's vision of "The Doomed Train," on p.p. 43-47; the account of Anna Kingsford's vision of Adonai, on pp. 64-68; the "Exhortation of Hermes to his Neophytes," on pp. 110-112; the verses "Concerning the Passage of the Soul," on pp. 169-170; and the illumination of Anna Kingsford concerning the "Work of Power," on pp. 180-181. I have also amplified the text in some places when, on comparing it with corresponding passages in "The Life of Anna Kingsford," I found that I could do so with advantage. These amplifications are not otherwise noted. Finally, I have added some notes where I thought that further explanation was desirable or would prove acceptable.

SAML. HOPGOOD HART.

Croydon, December, 1905.

INTRODUCTION.

There are certain introductory remarks which, in view of the prevailing tendency to reject prior to examination whatever conflicts with strongly cherished preconceptions—as anything purporting to be a "new Gospel" is undoubtedly calculated to do—may be made with advantage. Those remarks are as follows:—

(1) As its title implies[6], that which is propounded is not really a new Gospel, but one of Interpretation only, which is precisely what is admitted by all serious and thoughtful persons to be the supreme need of the times. It was said, for instance, by the late Matthew Arnold, "At the present moment there are two things about the Christian religion which must be obvious to every percipient person: one, that men cannot do without it; the other, that they cannot do with it as it is."

(2) As also its title implies[6] nothing new is told in it, but that only which is old is interpreted; and the appeal on its behalf is not to authority, whether of Book, Tradition, or Institution, but to the Understanding—a quality which accords not only with the spirit of the times, but also—as shewn herein—with that of religion itself, properly so called.

(3) Scripture manifestly comprises two conflicting systems of doctrine and practice, having for their representatives respectively the priest and the prophet, one only of which systems, and this the system reprobated in Scripture itself, has hitherto obtained recognition from Christendom. It is the purpose of the New Gospel of Interpretation to expound the system represented by the prophet and approved in Scripture, with a view to replacing the other.

(4) For those who attach value to the prophecies contained in the Bible, so far from there being an *a priori* improbability against the delivery of a new revelation in interpretation, confirmation, or completion of the former revelation, and in correction of the false presentment of it, the probability ought to be all in favour of such an event. This is because Scripture abounds in predictions of a restoration both of faculty and of knowledge, as to take place at the present time and under the existing conditions of Church and World; and this of such kind as shall constitute a second and spiritual manifestation of the Christ in rectification of the perversion of the import of His first and personal manifestation, and in arrest of the great Apostacy, not only from the true faith of Christ but from religion itself, of which that perversion has been the cause.

(5) So far from the idea of a new revelation which shall have for its end the disclosure, as the true sense of Scripture and Dogma, of a sense differing so widely from that hitherto accepted as to be virtually destructive of it,—so far from this idea being universally repugnant to orthodox ecclesiastics, it has found warm recognition from one of the foremost of modern churchmen. This is the late Cardinal Newman.

Said Dr Newman in his *Apologia pro vitâ suâ*, speaking of his earlier days, "The broad philosophy of Clement and Origen carried me away; the philosophy, not the theological doctrine.... Some portions of their teaching, magnificent in themselves, came like music to my inward ear, as if the response to ideas, which, with little external to encourage them, I had cherished so long. These were based on the mystical or sacramental principle, and spoke of the various Economies or Dispensations of the Eternal. I understood these passages to mean that the exterior world, physical and historical, was but the manifestation to our senses of realities greater than itself. Nature was a parable: Scripture was an allegory:..... The process of change had been slow; it had been done not rashly, but by rule and measure, 'at sundry times and in divers manners,' first one disclosure and then another, till the whole evangelical doctrine was brought into full manifestation. And thus room was made for the anticipation of further and deeper disclosures of truths still under the veil of the letter, and in their season to be revealed. The visible world still remains without its divine interpretation: Holy Church in her sacraments and her hierarchical appointments, will remain, even to the end of the world, after all but a symbol of those heavenly facts which fill eternity. Her mysteries are but the expressions, in human language, of truths to which the human mind is unequal"[7].

Dr Newman is credited also with the remark, made on visiting Rome for his investiture, that he saw no hope for religion save in a new revelation.

These are utterances the value of which is in no way diminished by the fact that their utterer failed to bring his own life into accordance with them. He could write, indeed, the hymn "Lead, kindly light"; but when the "kindly light" was vouchsafed him of those suggestions of a system of thought concealed within the Christian Symbology, "magnificent in themselves" and making "music to his inward ear," which he found in the patristic writings; instead of following that lead, and striving to exhume the treasures of divine truth thus buried and hidden from sight, for the salvation of a world perishing for want of them,—he turned his back upon it, and—entering the Church of Rome—wrote his "Grammar of Assent," calling upon others to follow him in committing the suicide, intellectual and moral, of renouncing the understanding and divorcing profession from conviction.

This was a catastrophe the explanation of which is not far to seek. Dr Newman had in him the elements which go to make both priest and prophet. But the former proved the stronger; and the Cain, the priest in him, suppressed the Abel, the prophet in him. Thus was he a type of the Church as hitherto she has been. But, happily, not as henceforth she will be. For "now is the Gospel of Interpretation come, and the kingdom of the Mother of God," even the "Woman," Intuition,—the mind's feminine mode, wherein it represents the perceptions and recollections of the Soul— who is ever "Mother of God" in man, and whose sons the prophets ever are, the greatest of them being called emphatically, for the fulness and purity of his intuition, the "Son of the Woman" and she a "virgin."

E.M.

CHAPTER I.
THE VOCATION.

My colleague in the work, the history of which I am about to render some account, was the late Anna Kingsford, *née* Bonus, M.D. of the University of Paris.

There was a link between her husband's family and mine, but we were not personally acquainted until, in the summer of 1873, she was led by reading one of my books[8] to open a correspondence with me, which disclosed so striking a community between us of ideas, aims, and methods, that I accepted an invitation to visit her at her husband's rectory at Pontesbury, Salop, in Shropshire, for the sake of a fuller discussion of them. This visit which lasted nearly a fortnight, took place in February, 1874[9].

The account I received of her history was in this wise. Born at Stratford, in Essex, on the 16th September, 1846, long after the last of her many brothers and sisters, and endowed with the most fragile of constitutions and liabilities the most distressing of bodily weakness and suffering, and differing widely, moreover, in temperament from all with whom she was associated, her young life had enjoyed but a scanty share of human sympathy, and was largely one of solitude and meditation, and such as to foster the highly artistic, idealistic, and mystic tendencies with which she was born. Singularly energetic of will, and conscious of powers both transcending in degree and differing in kind from any that she recognised in others, she assiduously exercised her faculties in many and various directions in the hope of discovering the special direction in which her mission lay. For, from her earliest childhood she had been conscious of a mission, for the accomplishment of which she had expressly come into the earth-life. And she claimed even to have distinct recollection of having been strongly dissuaded from coming, on account of the terrible suffering which awaited her in the event of her assuming a body of flesh. Indeed, so little conscious was she of the reality of her human parentage that she was wont to look upon herself as a suppositious child of fairy origin; and on her first visit to the pantomime, when the fairies made their appearance on the stage, she declared that they were her proper people, and cried and struggled to get to them with such vehemence that it was necessary to remove her from the theatre. Among her amusements, her chief delight was in the ample gardens around her homes at Stratford and Blackheath, where she would hold familiar converse with the flowers, putting into their petals tiny notes for her lost relatives, the fairies, who in return would visit her in her dreams and assure her of their continued affection, and counsel her to have patience and courage.

The chief occupation of her girlhood was the writing of poems and tales[10] which were tinged with an exquisite mysticism, and showed a ripeness of soul and maturity of feeling and knowledge wholly unaccountable for by her years, her experiences, or her physical heredity. At school she always obtained the first prizes for composition, and her faculty of improvisation was the delight of her companions; the subjects of these her earlier romances being lovely princesses, gallant knights, castles, dragons, and the like, when—as may readily be supposed—her tall and slender frame, long golden hair, delicacy of complexion, deep-set hazel eyes, beauty of feature, the brow and the mouth being especially notable, the brightness of her looks, vivacity of her manner, her musical voice, and the easy eloquence of her diction,—all combined to make her an ideal heroine for her own romances. She could hardly, however, be said to be a *persona grata* with her pastors and masters. For while her independence of character and strength of will were apt to bring her into conflict with rules and regulations of which she failed to recognise the need, her thirst for knowledge, especially on religious subjects, prompted her to the proposition of questions which were highly embarrassing to her teachers; and nothing that they could say succeeded in convincing her that her duty lay in believing what she was told, and not in understanding it. She very early learnt to resent the disabilities of her sex, and to insist that they were not real but artificial, the result of masculine selfishness and injustice. This hatred of injustice and its correlative cruelty, especially towards animals, attained in her the force and dignity of a passion, her sensitiveness on this score making the chief mental misery of her life.

Of one gift possessed by her she early learnt to repress the manifestation. This was the faculty for seeing apparitions and divining the characters and fortunes of people. For she was a born seer. But the inability of her elders to comprehend the faculty, and their consequent ascription of it to pathological causes, were wont to lead to references to the family doctor with results so eminently disagreeable and even injurious to her, as soon to suggest the wisdom of keeping silence respecting her experiences.

Her first published compositions were written at the age of thirteen[11], the editors who accepted her contributions to their magazines being under the impression that they came from a grown-up person and not from the mere child that she was. They cost her, she assured me, little labour, especially the poems, but seemed to come to her ready-made, and to flow through her spontaneously. And whatever the country in which their scene lay, the local colouring and descriptions were always faithful and vivid, as if the places and their inhabitants were familiar and even actually visible to her.

It was not, however, to any encouragement of her peculiar gifts that such excellency as she exhibited was due. Rather were they severely repressed, especially in respect of drawing, singing and music, lest she should be tempted to follow them as a profession; a fear which had been excited by the suggestions of her masters that she would be certain of success in any of those lines.

Her innate consciousness of a mission seemed to her to indicate her as destined for some redemptive work, not only for others, but also for herself. For, while the instincts of the Champion and the Saviour were potent in her, she was dimly conscious of its possessing also an expiatory element, in virtue of which her own salvation would largely depend upon her endeavours to save others. She had as yet no theory whereby to explain this or any other of the problems she was to herself. All that she knew was that she possessed, or rather was possessed of, these feelings and impulses. It was easy to see by her account of herself that she was as one driven of the Spirit long before the Spirit definitely revealed itself to her. The two departments of humanity which she felt especially impelled to succour and save were her own sex and the animals. For she would recognise no hard and fast line between masculine and feminine, human and animal, or even between animal and plant. In her eyes everything that lived was humanity, only in different stages of its unfoldment. Even the flowers were persons for her.

As she approached womanhood she found herself looking forward to marriage far less for its own sake than as a means of emancipation from restrictions on her choice of a career. Her father died while she was yet wanting two or three years of her majority, leaving her mistress of an income ample for a single woman. And when at length she became engaged to Algernon Godfrey Kingsford, a cousin to whom she had some time been attached, it was on the understanding that she should remain unfettered in this respect. He held at the time a post in the Civil Service; but soon after their marriage, which took place on the last day of 1867, determined to read for holy orders. This gave her an opportunity for making herself acquainted with Anglican theology, of which—thirsting for knowledge of all kinds—she eagerly availed herself, accompanying him in all his studies, and greatly facilitating them by her admirable scholarly methods. This proved to be the first great step in her religious and intellectual training for her destined mission.

One of the occupations of her early married life was the editing of a lady's magazine, which she purchased with a view of making it an instrument for the dissemination of her ideas especially in regard to her sex. And she accordingly took an active part in the movement then recently originated for the enfranchisement of women, achieving an extraordinary success as a public speaker. But, becoming convinced that their cause would be best advanced by the practical demonstration of their fitness for the promotion they sought, and also feeling her own need for the discipline of a severe intellectual training to balance the emotional side of her nature, she soon withdrew from active participation in the movement. She moreover recognised as a grave mistake the disposition evinced by her fellow-workers to suppress their womanliness in favour of a factitious masculinity, under the impression that they would thereby exalt their sex; her idea being, that their true policy lay in magnifying rather than in depreciating their womanhood. Meanwhile she had given birth to a daughter, her only child.

Her magazine was given up after a couple of years, the results failing to justify the expenditure of time, labour and money, requisite for its continuance. Not that it lacked adequate support; but the principles on which she insisted on conducting it proved to be incompatible with commercial success. She resolutely refused all advertisements of articles, whether of food or of clothing, of which she disapproved; and she had adopted the pythagorean regimen and discarded as unhygienic sundry articles of attire ordinarily deemed indispensable by her sex. It was in her magazine that she first struck the note which proved the initiation of the holy warfare since waged against the horrors of the physiological laboratory, a warfare in which she bore a foremost part and developed the malady of which she died.

In 1870, a long and severe illness, which compelled her return to her mother's house at Hastings to be nursed, led to her entry upon another phase in her inner life, and a further stage in the process of her education for her mission. She had early recoiled from the faith in which she had been reared. This was Protestantism in its most unlovely form, cold, harsh, narrow, dogmatic. Her closer acquaintance with it as a clergyman's wife had done nothing to mitigate her judgment of it. Explaining nothing and lacking fervour and poetry, it left head and heart alike unsatisfied. Her residence as an invalid at Hastings brought her into intimacy with some devout Catholics, the effect of which was to intensify the repugnance already set up. She attended the Catholic services, and visited the sisters in the convent, reading their books of devotion and even making an extended study of Catholic doctrine, for she would do nothing by halves. She found what satisfied her heart and artistic tastes. But the chief determining cause of the change upon which she at length resolved, was her reception by night of sundry visitations, purporting to be of angelic nature, and enjoining on her, for the sake of the mission to which she was called—the knowledge of which, she was told, would in due time be revealed to her—that she join the Roman communion. Well aware that the confession of such experiences, whether to her relations or to a minister of her own Church, would elicit only a smile of pity or contempt, with a recommendation to seek medical advice, and involve other contingencies equally distasteful, she resolved to see how the same confession would be treated by a Catholic priest. The result of the essay was that she was listened to with respect and sympathy, and informed that the Church fully recognised such visitations as coming within the divine order, and as being a token of high spiritual favour and grace; and while it refrained from pronouncing positively on them, considered that they ought not to be lightly disregarded. She was soon afterwards received into the Roman Church, being baptised on September 14, 1870. On June 9, 1872, she was confirmed by Archbishop Manning, who admonished her to utilise her attractions in making converts. And on each occasion she received additional names, in virtue of which she now bore the names of all the five women who were by the Cross and at the Sepulchre.

None the less, however, did she retain her independence of mind and conduct. She accepted no direction, and professed no tenet that she did not understand. And it was soon made clear to her that the Spirit, of whom she was being impelled, did not intend her to regard her adoption of Catholicism as more than a step in her education for the work required of her. For the following year saw her bent on seeking a medical degree, under the impression that such a step was in some way related to the mission of which she had received such and so many mysterious intimations. And she had scarcely commenced her study of medicine when this impression was reinforced by the following incident, the scene of which was her home in Shropshire, in the parish of which her husband had then recently become incumbent, and where I first visited them.

This was the receipt of a letter from a lady who was a stranger to her, written from a distant part of the country, and saying that she, the writer, had read with profound interest and admiration a story[12] of Mrs Kingsford which, after appearing in her magazine, had been published as a book, and that after reading it she had received from the Holy Spirit a message for her which was to be delivered in person. After some hesitation as to what reply to make, Mrs Kingsford—whose account I am following exactly—agreed to receive her; an appointment was made, and the stranger duly presented herself. She was tall, erect, distinguished looking, with hair of iron-grey and strangely brilliant eyes, and was perfectly calm and collected of demeanour. The message was to the effect that Mrs Kingsford was to remain in retirement for five years, continuing the studies and mode of life on which she had entered, whatever they might be—for that the messenger did not know—and to suffer nothing and no one to draw her aside from them. That when these probationary five years were past, the Holy Spirit would bring her forth from her seclusion, and a great work would be given her to do. All this was uttered with a rapt and inspired expression, as though she had been a Sibyl pronouncing an oracle. After delivering her message, the messenger kissed her on both cheeks and departed, first asking only whether she thought her mad; a question to which for a moment Mrs Kingsford found it somewhat difficult to make reply. But only for a moment. For then there rushed on her the conviction that it was all genuine and true, and was but a fresh unfoldment of the mystery of her life and destiny, and in full accordance with her own foreshadowings from the beginning.

Some four years later, at a time when Mrs Kingsford was in great straits for want of a suitable home in London in which to carry on her studies, the same lady was similarly commissioned on her behalf, while totally ignorant both of her whereabouts and her need, and with results entirely satisfactory. On which occasion I had the privilege of making her acquaintance, and the satisfaction of finding her not merely perfectly sane, but a person entitled to the highest consideration, noted for her pious devotion to works of beneficence involving complete self-abnegation; and in short a veritable "Mother in Israel."

The event above related occurred in the spring of 1873, the summer of which year saw Mrs Kingsford impelled to do what led to the most crucial of the events upon which her destined mission hinged, namely, to write to me the letter which led to my visit to her home. In the autumn of the same year she passed her matriculation examination at the Apothecaries' Hall with success so great as to fill her with high hopes of a triumphant passage through the course of her student-life. But immediately afterwards her hopes were dashed, for the English medical authorities saw fit to close their schools to women, and the way to her anticipated career was shut against her.

Such was the position when, in February, 1874, I visited the Shropshire rectory, and such in brief the history which was gradually unfolded to me as my evident sympathy and appreciation gained the confidence of the still young couple, whose senior I was by some twenty years. Both husband and wife were at their wits' end, the situation being aggravated by a circumstance which was first brought to my knowledge on my suggestion of the postponement of her design until such time as the medical authorities should come to their right minds and re-open their schools to women. The circumstance in question was her terrible liability on the ground of ill-health, and especially of asthma, to which she was a martyr, life in the country being impossible to her for the greater part of the year, when it was only in some large city that she was able to breathe. With the schools closed against her in England, her thoughts turned towards France, the University of Paris being open to women. But for obvious reasons her husband, who could not absent himself from his duties to accompany her, would not consent to her going thither unless under suitable protection. For himself he had but one wish, that she should follow her bent and fashion her life as seemed best to her; for he recognised her as entitled by her endowments and aspirations, as well as by the terms of their engagement, to full liberty of action, while the conditions of her health claimed all consideration from him. If, indeed, the Gods had destined her for a mission requiring freedom of action combined with the shelter and support of a husband's name, it seemed to me that in him they had created a man expressly for the office. For some time, however, the difficulty seemed insuperable, and one that would yield to no amount of deliberation, even with the best will of all concerned.

Meanwhile her self-revelations continued, being evidently prompted, at least as much by the desire to obtain some explanation of herself for herself, to whom she was, she avowed, a complete puzzle, as by the desire to elicit answering confidences from me. And they became with each disclosure more and more striking, until I could hardly resist the conviction that she was possessed of some faculty in virtue of which she was able to have direct perception of conclusions to which I had won my way by dint of long and arduous thinking, and in some instances in advance of me. She had read my mental history between the lines of my books, and was fully prepared to learn that I too had a consciousness, analogous to her own, of a mission in life perhaps also analogous to her own.

This, I was able to assure her, was indeed the case, and that all my books had been written in the idea of finding my way to it by dint of free, unfettered thinking. For, brought up in the strictest of evangelical sects, I had even as a lad begun to be revolted by the creed in which I was reared, and had very early come to regard its tenets, especially of total depravity and vicarious atonement, as a libel nothing short of blasphemous against both God and man, and to feel that no greater boon could be bestowed on the world than its emancipation from the bondage of a belief so degrading and so destructive of any lofty ideal. I had felt strongly that only in such measure as I might be the means of its abolition would my life be a success and a satisfaction to myself. It even seemed to me that my own credit was involved in the matter; and that in disproving such beliefs I should be vindicating my own character. For if God were evil, as those doctrines made Him, I could by no possibility be good, since I must have my derivation from Him. And I knew that, however weak and unwise I might be, I was not evil.

Then, too, my life, like hers, had been one of much isolation and meditation. I had felt myself a stranger even with my closest intimates. For I was always conscious of a difference which separated me from them, and of a side to which they could not have access. I had graduated at Cambridge with the design of taking orders; but only to find that I could not do so conscientiously, and to feel that to commit myself to any conditions incompatible with absolute freedom of thought and expression would be a treachery against both myself and my kind;—for it was for no merely personal end that I wanted to discover the truth. I longed to get away from all my surroundings in order, first, to think myself out of all that I had been taught, and so to make my mind as a clean sheet whereon to receive true impressions and at first hand; and, next, to think myself into a condition and to a level wherein I could see all things—myself, nature, and God—face to face, with vision undimmed and undistorted by beliefs which, being inherited only and traditional, instead of the result of conviction honestly arrived at, were factitious and unreal; no living outcome of my own growth and observation, but a veritable straitwaistcoat, stifling life and restraining development. And so it had come that—as related in my first novel, "The Pilgrim and the Shrine"[13], which was essentially autobiographical—I had eagerly fallen in with a proposal to join an expedition to the then newly-discovered placers of California, an enterprise which, besides promising to gratify the love for adventure, physical as well as mental, which was strong in me, would postpone if not solve the difficulty of my position. It possessed, moreover, the high recommendation of taking me to the world of the fresh, unsophisticated West, instead of to that East which had been made almost hateful to me by its association with the tenets by which existence had been poisoned for me.

So, setting my face towards the sunset, I became one of the band of "Forty-niners" in California, and remained abroad in the continents and isles of the Pacific, from America passing to Australia, until the intended year of my absence had grown into nearly ten years, and I had experienced well-nigh every vicissitude and extreme which might serve to heighten the consciousness, toughen the fibre, and try the soul of man. But throughout all, the idea of a mission remained with me, gathering force and consistency, until it was made clear to me that not destruction merely, but construction, not the exposure of error but the demonstration of truth, was comprised in it. For I saw that it was possible to reduce religion to a series of first principles, necessary truths and self-evident propositions, and that only in such measure as it was thus reduced and discerned, was it really true and really believed;—in short, that faith and knowledge are identical. To accept a religion on the ground that one had been born in it, and apart from its appeal to the mind and moral conscience, and thus to make it dependent upon the accident of birth and parentage, was to resemble the African savage who for the same reason worships Mumbo Jumbo. How, moreover,—I asked myself—could a religion which was not in accord with first principles, represent a God, Who, to be God, must Himself be the first of, and must comprise all principles; must account logically for all the facts of consciousness, be it unfolded as far as it may? Granting that, as the poet says, "an honest man's the noblest work of God," it was for me no less true that "an honest God's the noblest work of man." And it was precisely such a being that I longed to elaborate out of, or discover in, my own consciousness, confident that the achievement meant the solution of all problems, the rectification of all difficulties, the satisfaction of all aspirations, intellectual, moral, and spiritual. Following such trains of thought, I arrived at the assurance that I had within my own consciousness both the truth itself and the verification of the truth, and that it remained only to find these.

Returning to England in 1857, and, after an interval, devoting myself to literature, all that I wrote, whether essay or fiction, represented the endeavour by probing the consciousness to the utmost in every direction to discover a central, radiant, and indefeasible point from which all things could be deduced, and on which, as a pivot they must depend and revolve. I read largely, and went much among people, always in search of aid in my quest; but only with the result of finding that neither from books nor from persons could I even begin to get what I sought, but only from thought.

Meanwhile everything seemed ordered with a view to the end ultimately attained. For, so far from having left behind me for ever the vicissitudes, and struggles, and trials, and ordeals, in which the wildernesses of the western and southern worlds had been so fruitful, I was found of them in the old world to which I had returned; and this in number, kind, and degree, such as to make it appear as if what I had borne before had been inflicted expressly for the purpose of enabling me to bear what was put upon me now. And it was only when I had learnt by experience that the very capacity for thought is enhanced by feeling no less than by thinking, that the "ministry of pain" found its explanation. For the feeling required of me proved to be that of the inner, not merely of the outer man, of the soul, not merely of the body; and the faculty, to be the intuition, and not merely the intellect. Hence I was made to learn by experience, long before the fact was formulated for me in words, that only "by the bruising of the outer, the inner is set free," and "man is alive only so far as he has felt."

Everything seemed contrived expressly in order to force me in this inward direction. Even in my literary work, nothing of the "trade" element was permitted to intrude. I could not write except when writing to or from my own centre. Faculty itself was shut off, if turned to any other purpose. Everything I wrote must minister to and represent a step in my own unfoldment.

I can confidently affirm that the only books which really helped me were, with scarcely an exception, those which I wrote myself. Of the exceptions the chief was Emerson. His essays had been my *vade mecum* in all my world-wide wanderings. And there were three sentences of his which, to use his own phrase, "found" me as no others had done. They were these: "The talent is the call"; "I the imperfect adore my own perfect"; and, "Beware when God lets loose a thinker on the earth." Like Emerson himself, I had yet to learn that man's own perfect is God, and self-culture is God-culture, provided the self be the inmost self. The two other books which most helped me were Bailey's "Festus," and Carlyle's "Hero-Worship." And I owed something to Tucker's "Light of Nature." By which it will be seen that my affinity was always for the prophets rather than the priests of literature; for the intuitionalists rather than the externalists.

Gradually two leading ideas took definite form in my mind, which, however, proved to be but two aspects or applications of one and the same idea. And that idea proved to be the keynote of all that I was seeking after. For it finally solved the problems of existence, of religion, of the Bible, of Being itself. Hence the necessity of this reference to it.

This idea was that of a duality subsisting in every unity, such as I had nowhere read or heard of. I was, of course, aware that the theological doctrine of the Trinity involved a Duality. But not of a kind to find a response in my mind. And being unable to assimilate it as it stood, I ignored it; putting it aside until it should present itself to me in an aspect in which it was intelligible. I felt, however vaguely, that the Duality I sought was in the Bible, though it had been missed by the official expositors of that book. And the conviction that it was in some way connected with my life-work was so strong that I constructed for the covers of my two first books a monogram symbolical of Genesis i. 27. And I looked to the unfoldment of what I felt to be the secret significance of that utterance for the explication of all the mysteries the solution of which engrossed me. The thought did not seem to originate in any of my experiences, but rather to be part of my original stock of innate ideas, supposing that there are such ideas, and to derive confirmation and explanation from my experiences.

Those experiences were in this wise. It had been my privilege to have the friendship of several women of a type so noble that to know them was at once an education and a religion; women whose perfection of character had served more than anything else to make me believe in God, when all other grounds had failed. I could in no wise account for them on the hypothesis of a fortuitous concourse of unintelligent atoms. And not only did I find that the higher the type the more richly they were endowed with precisely the faculty of which I myself was conscious as distinguishing me from my fellows; I found also that I was unable to recognise any woman as of a high type as woman save in so far as she was possessed of it. I had failed to find any who possessed the knowledge I craved, and who were thereby able to help me in my thought. They helped me nevertheless, but it was by *being* what they were, rather than by *knowing* and *doing*, be they admirable as they might in these respects. I recognised in them that which supplemented and complemented my mental self in such wise as to suggest unbounded possibilities of results to accrue from the intimate association of two minds thus attuned to each other, and duly unfolded by thought and study. It needed, it seemed to me, but the reverberation and intensification of thought, induced by the apposition of two minds thus related, for the production of the divine child Truth in the very highest spheres of thought. So that the results would by no means be restricted to the mere sum of the associated capacities of the two minds themselves. And in view of such high possibilities I found myself appropriating and applying the ejaculation which Virgil puts into the mouth of Anna when urging the union of her sister Dido with Æneas—

"Quæ surgere regna

Conjugio tali!"

and I felt with Tennyson that

> "They two together well might move the world."

So boundless seemed to me the kingdoms of Truth, Goodness, and Beauty which would spring from such conjunction.

It goes without saying that such relationship was contemplated by me only as the accompaniment of a happy re-marriage. [For I had married in Australia only to be widowered after a year's wedlock.] But such a prospect was so long withheld as to make me dubious of its realisation[14]. Nevertheless, some inner voice was ever saying: "Wait; wait. Everything comes to him who waits, provided only he do so in faith and patience, looking to the highest." But that I did wait, and accordingly kept myself free for what ultimately was assigned to me, was due far less to the expectation of finding that for which I waited, than to the vivid consciousness which I had of the bitterness that would come of finding it, only to be withheld from it through a previous disposal of myself in some other and incompatible quarter. This was an impression which served largely to keep my life as free as I desired my thought to be. But that the as yet undisclosed arbiters of my destiny deemed it insufficient as a deterrent, appeared from their reinforcement of it in a manner which effectually debarred me from marriage save on the condition, impossible to me, of a mercenary alliance. This was a reversal of fortune through a succession of losses so serious as to be the cause of reducing my means to the minimum compatible with existence at all in my own station, which soon afterwards happened. That there were yet further reasons for this imposition on me of the rule of poverty, arising out of the nature of the work required of me, was in due time made manifest, and also what those reasons were. They need not be specified here, excepting only this one. It made impossible the ascription to my destined colleague of mercenary motives for her association with me. In this I came to recognise a delicate providence for which I felt I could not be too thankful. In the meantime, even while smarting severely from this dispensation, and others yet more bitter which were heaped on me for no apparent cause or fault of my own that I could discern, the thought that most of all served to sustain me under what I felt would have utterly broken down in heart or head, or in both of these organs, any other person whatever of whom I had knowledge,—that thought was the surmise or suspicion that all these things, hard to bear as they were, and undeserved as they seemed, might prove to be blessings in disguise, in ministering to the realisation of the controlling ambition of my life by educating me for it; and that according to the manner in which I bore them might be the result.

There is yet one more personal disclosure essential to this part of my relation. It concerns my own mental standpoint at the time at which my narrative has arrived. Bent as I was on penetrating the secret of things at first hand, and by means of a thought absolutely free, I was never for a moment disposed to turn, as my so-called free-thinking contemporaries one and all had turned, a scornful back upon whatever related to or savoured of the current religion. Scripture and dogma were not for me necessarily either false or inscrutable because their official exponents had presented them in an aspect which outraged my reason and revolted my conscience. I felt bound—if only in justice to them and myself—at least to find out what they did mean before finally discarding them. And in this act of justice I was strangely sustained by a sense of the possibility that the truth, if any, contained in them, was no other than that of which I was in search. This is to say, that in all my investigations I kept before me the idea that, if I could discern the actual nature of existence and the intended sense of the Bible and Christianity, independently of each other, they might prove on comparison to be identical; in which case the latter would really represent a true revelation. Meanwhile, I found myself constrained to believe, as an axiomatic proposition, that the higher and nobler the conception I framed in my imagination of the nature of existence, and the more in accordance with my ideas of what, to be perfect, the constitution of the universe ought to be, the nearer I should come to the actual truth.

Similarly with religion. For a religion to be true, it must, I felt absolutely assured, be ideally perfect after the most perfect ideal that we can frame. This is to say, that not only must it be in itself such as to satisfy both head and heart, mind and moral conscience, spirit and soul; it must also be perfectly simple, obviously reasonable, coherent, self-evident, founded in the nature of things, incapable—when once comprehended—of being conceived of as otherwise, absolutely equitable, eternally true, and recognisable as being all these, invariable in operation, independent of all accidents of time, place, persons and events, and comparable to the demonstration of a mathematical problem in that it needs no testimony or authority beyond those of the mind; and requiring for its efficacious observance, nothing that is extraneous or inaccessible to the subject-individual, but within his ability to recognise and fulfil, provided only that he so will. It must also be such as to enable him by the observance of it to turn his existence to the highest possible account imaginable by him, be his imagination as developed as it may: and all this as independently of any being other than himself, as if he were the sole personal entity in the universe, and were himself the universe. That is to say, the means of a man's perfectionment must inhere in his own system, and he must be competent of himself effectually to apply them. It is further necessary, because equitable, that he be allowed sufficient time and opportunity for the discovery, understanding and application of such means.

Such are the terms and conditions of an ideally perfect religion, as I conceived of them. It is a definition which excludes well-nigh, if not quite, all the characteristics ordinarily regarded as appertaining to religion, and notably to that of Christendom. For in excluding everything extraneous to the actual subject-individual, and requiring religion to be self-evident and necessarily true, it excludes as superfluous and irrelevant, history, tradition, authority, revelation, as ordinarily conceived of, ecclesiastical ordinance, priestly ministration, mediatorial function, vicarious satisfaction, and even the operation of Deity as subsisting without and apart from the man, all of which are essential elements in the accepted conception of religion. Nevertheless, profound as was my distrust of the faithfulness of the orthodox presentation, I could not reconcile myself to a renunciation of the originals on which that presentation was founded, until I had satisfied myself that I had fathomed their intended and real meaning.

I had, moreover, very early conceived a personal affection for Jesus as a man, so strong as to serve as a deterrent both from abandoning the faith founded on Him, and from accepting it as it is as worthy of Him.

Such was my standpoint, intellectual and religious, at the period in question. The time came when it found full justification; our results being such as to verify it in everyone of its manifold aspects. And not this only. The doctrine which had so mysteriously evolved itself out of my consciousness to attain by slow degrees the position of a controlling influence in my life, the doctrine, namely of a Duality subsisting in the Original Unity of Underived Being, and as inhering therefore in every unit of derived being, this doctrine proved to be the key to the mysteries both of Creation and of Redemption, as propounded in the Bible and manifested in the Christ; the key also to the nature of man, disclosing the facts both of his possession of divine potentialities as his birthright, and his endowment with the faculty whereby to discern and to realise them. And while it proved constructive in respect of Divine Truth, it proved destructive in respect of the falsification of that truth which had passed for orthodoxy, by disclosing the source, the motive, the method and the agents of that falsification.

But these things were still in the future. At the time with which we are now concerned, I had commenced a book to represent the standpoint just described, "The Keys of the Creeds." The first and initial draft of that book was written under the sympathetic eye of one of the order of noble women to which reference has been made, and owed much to the enhancement of faculty derived by me from such conjunction of minds. The second and final draft was written under like relationship with another member of the self-same order, even she who proved to be my destined collaborator in the work of which this book recounts the story. It was published in 1875. It is necessary only to say further of the book thus produced, that notwithstanding certain defects of expression, due chiefly to an insufficient acquaintance with the terminology of metaphysics, it proved an invaluable help to very many, as was amply shown by the letters of grateful appreciation received from them by me. The keynote was that which afterwards found expression in the utterance,—

"There is no enlightenment from without: the secret of things is revealed from within.

"From without cometh no Divine Revelation: but the Spirit within beareth witness"[15].

For the lesson it contained was the lesson that the phenomenal world cannot disclose its own secret. To find this, man must seek in that substantial world which lies within himself, since all that is real is within the man. From which it followed that if there is no within, or if that within be inaccessible, either there is no reality, or man has no organon of knowledge, and is by constitution agnostic. Meanwhile, the very fact of my possession of an ideal exempt from the limitations of the apparent, constituted for me a strong presumption in favour of the reality of the ideal.

The moment of contact between my destined colleague and myself, was as critical for one as for the other, only that in my case the crisis was intellectual. I could see to the end of the argument I was then elaborating; and that it landed me close to the dividing barrier between the two worlds of sense and spirit, supposing the latter to have any being[16]. But I neither saw beyond, nor knew how to ascertain whether or not there is a beyond. We were discussing the question of there being an inner sense in Scripture, such as my book suggested; and whether, supposing it to have such a sense, it required for its discernment any faculty more recondite than a subtle imagination; and if it did, is there such a faculty? and what is its nature? By which it will be seen that I was still in ignorance of the nature of the faculty I found in myself and recognised as especially subsisting in women, and which, for me, really made the woman.

The reply rendered by her to these questionings constituted the proof positive that I had at length discovered the mind which my own had so long craved as its sorely needed complement. In response to them she gave me a manuscript in her own writing, asking me to read it and tell her frankly what I thought of it. Having read and re-read it, I enquired how and where she had got it. She replied by asking what I thought of it. I answered, "If there is such a thing as divine revelation, I know of nothing that comes nearer to my ideal of what it ought to be. It is exactly what the world is perishing for want of—a reasonable faith." She then told me that it had come to her in her sleep, but whence or how she did not know; nor could she say whether she had seen it or heard it, but only that it came suddenly into her mind, without her having ever heard or thought of such teaching before. It was an exposition of the Story of the Fall, exhibiting it as a parable having a significance purely spiritual, wholly reasonable, and of universal application, physical persons, things, and events described in it disappearing in favour of principles, processes, and states appertaining to the soul; no mere local history, therefore, but an eternal verity. The experience, she went on to tell me, was far from exceptional; she had received many things which had greatly struck and pleased her in the same way, and sometimes while in the waking state in a sort of day-dream. It was subsequently incorporated into our book, "The Perfect Way."

Her account of her faculty, of which she related several instances, produced a profound impression on me. It differed altogether from any that I had heard of as claimed by the votaries of "Spiritualism," a creed to which neither of us had assented; such little experience as we had of it having failed to convince us of the genuineness of its phenomena; though she, on her part, confessed to having been somewhat at a loss to account for some things she had seen. But though not spiritualists, we were not materialists. Rather were we idealists, who had yet to learn and, as the event proved, were destined shortly to learn, that the Ideal *is* the Real, and is Spiritual.

The event also proved that in order to learn it and to know it positively by experience, there were two conditions to be fulfilled, on both of which she had already entered, but I had yet to enter. One of these conditions was physical, the other was emotional. The former consisted in the renunciation of flesh-food in favour of a diet derived from the vegetable kingdom. The latter condition consisted in the kindling of our enthusiasm for the ideal into a flame of such ardour and intensity as to make it the dominant passion of our lives, and one in which all others would be swallowed up. It was to be an enthusiasm at once for Humanity, for Perfection, for God.

Had we been in any degree instructed in spiritual or occult science, we should have known that the renunciation of flesh-food, though in itself a physical act, has ever been recognised by initiates as the prime essential in the unfoldment of the spiritual faculties; since only when man is purely nourished can he attain clearness and fulness of spiritual perception. As it was, neither of us had ever heard of occult science, or of the necessity of such a regimen to the perfectionment of faculty. She had adopted it on grounds physiological, chemical, hygienic, æsthetic, and moral; not on grounds mental or spiritual. I now undertook to adopt it partly on the same grounds which had influenced her, and partly with a view to enhance and consolidate the sympathy subsisting between us. The mental and spiritual advantages of the regimen made themselves known to us by experience.

The other condition found its fulfilment through the knowledge I derived from her of the methods of the physiologists. That savages, sorcerers, brigands, religious fanatics, and corrupt priesthoods had always been wont to make torture their gain or their pastime, I was well aware, and believed that evolution would sweep them and their practices away in its course. But the discovery now first made to me that identical barbarities are systematically perpetrated by the leaders of modern science on the pretext of benefiting humanity, in an age which claims to represent the summit of such evolution as has yet been accomplished; and that after all its boasts, the best that science can do for the world is to convert it into a hell and its population into fiends, by the deliberate renunciation of the distinctive sentiments of humanity,—this was a discovery which filled me with unspeakable horror and amazement, at once raising to a white heat the enthusiasm of love for the ideal already kindled within me, and adding to it a like enthusiasm of detestation for its opposite. From which it came that I found myself under the impulsion simultaneously of two mighty influences, the one attracting, the other repelling, but both operating in the same direction. For while by the former I was drawn upwards by the beauty of an ideal indefinitely enhanced by its contrast with the foul actual below, by the latter I was impelled upwards by the hideousness of that actual. The sight of the moral abyss disclosed to me in Vivisection, as I perused volume after volume of the annals of the practice written by the perpetrators themselves, and now first made accessible to me, effectually purged out of my system any particle of dilettanteism that might have still lurked in it, compelling me to regard as of the utmost urgency all and more than all that I had hitherto contemplated doing deliberately.

This was the construction of a system of thought which by force of its appeal to both those two indispensable constituents of humanity, the head and the heart, shall compel acceptance from all persons really human, and in presence of which the whole system of which Vivisection was the typical outcome and symbol should vanish from off the earth. This system was Materialism of which only now did I discern the full significance. The systematic organisation of wholesale, protracted, uncompensatable torture, for ends purely selfish, was—I saw with absolute distinctness—not an accidental and avoidable outcome of Materialism, but its logical and inevitable outcome. And it was to the eradication of Materialism that, from that moment, I dedicated myself. It was a rescue work for both man and beast, seeing that humanity itself was menaced with extinction. For the materialist, of course, that which makes the man is the form. For me it was the character, and it was this, the character of mankind present and to come, that was at stake. For man demonised is no longer man. In the overthrow of Materialism, I saw absolutely, was salvation alone to be found, whether for man or beast. The consideration that only as an abstainer from flesh-food I could with entire consistency contend against vivisection, was a potent factor in determining my change of diet. True, the distinction between death and torture was a broad one. But the statistics I now for the first time perused, of the slaughter-house and the cattle-traffic, showed beyond question, that torture, and this prolonged and severe, is involved in the use of animals for food as well as for science. And over and above this was the instinctive perception of the probability that neither would they who had them killed, whether for food, for sport, or for clothing, be allowed the privilege of rescuing them from the hands of the physiologist; nor would the animals be allowed to accept their deliverance at the hands of those who thus used them. They who would save others, we felt, must first make sacrifice in themselves. And in the presence of the joy of working to effect such salvation, sacrifice would cease to be sacrifice.

This, too, we noted, and with no small satisfaction—that to make the rescue of the animals an immediate and urgent motive, was in no way to abandon the original motive of hatred to the tenet of vicarious atonement. For we recognised vivisection itself as but the extension to the domain of science, of the very principle by which we had been inexpressibly revolted in the domain of religion;—the principle of seeking one's own salvation by the sacrifice of another, and that the innocent. And so we learnt that "New Scientist is but Old Priest writ differently,"—to vary Milton's expression; and that in both domains the tenet had its root in Materialism. When the time came for our mission to be more particularly defined, our satisfaction was unbounded on receiving the charge, "We mean you to lay bare the secrets of the world's sacrificial system." It expressed with absolute conciseness and exactitude all that we had in our minds, far better than we could have expressed it.

The importance of this question of vivisection in vitalising us for the work before us, will be seen by the following fact. The time came when we knew that the work committed to us was that revelation anew of the Christ which was to constitute His Second Advent, inasmuch as it was the interpretation of the truth of which He was the manifestation. It was to be a spiritual coming; in the "clouds of heaven," the heaven of the "kingdom within" of man's restored understanding. And, as at His first advent so at His second, He was to have His birth among the animals.

And so it verily was. For—as I have elsewhere stated—"Their terrible wrongs, culminating at the hands of their scientific tormentors, were the last drops which filled to overflowing with anguish, indignation and wrath, hearts already brimming with the sense of the world's degradation and misery, wringing from them the cry which rent the heavens for His descent, and in direct and immediate response to which He came.

"For the New Gospel of Interpretation was vouchsafed in express recognition of the determined endeavour, by means of a thought absolutely fearless and free, to scale the topmost heights, fathom the lowest depths, and penetrate to the inmost recesses of Consciousness, in search of the solution of the problem of Existence, under the assured conviction that, when found, it would prove to be one that would make above all things Vivisection impossible, if only by demonstrating the constitution of things to be such that, terrible as is the lot of the victims of the practice here, they are not without compensation hereafter, while the lot of their tormentors will be unspeakably worse than even that of their victims here. And so it proved, with absolute certainty to be the case, to the full vindication at the same time of the Divine Justice and the Divine Love;" no experience being withheld which would qualify us to bear positive testimony thereto. For, although at the outset we were, as I have said, in no wise believers in the possibility of such experiences, the time came, and came quickly, when the veil was withdrawn, and the secrets of the Beyond were disclosed to us in plenitude, in its every sphere, from the abyss of hell to the heights of heaven. And we learnt that this had become possible through the passionate energy with which, in our search for the highest truth, for the highest ends, and in purest love to redeem, we had directed our thought inwards and upwards, living at the same time the life requisite to qualify us for such perceptions. Thus did we obtain practical realisation of the promise that they who do the divine will, by living the divine life, shall know of the divine doctrine. Our whole mental attitude had been one of prayer in its essential sense; which is not that of *saying* prayers, but as it came to be defined for us—"the intense direction of the will and desire towards the Highest; an unchanging intent to know nothing but the Highest." Because "to think inwardly, to pray intensely, and to imagine centrally, is to hold converse with God." And we had done this without knowing it was prayer, or calling it by that name. For, knowing only the conventional conception of prayer, we had recoiled from it as from other conventional conceptions of things religious.

Now, however, we found that we had done instinctively and spontaneously precisely what was necessary to bring us into relations at once with our spiritual selves and with the world of those who consist only of the spiritual self. For, by thus becoming vitalised and sensitive in that part of man's system which endures and passes on, we had come into open conditions with the world of those who have thus endured and passed on, and are no longer of the terrestrial, but of the celestial, having surmounted all lower and intermediate planes. All this came to us without anticipation on our part, or any conscious seeking for it; but yet without causing dismay or surprise when it came. For it came so gradually as to seem to be but the natural and orderly result of the unfoldment of our own spiritual consciousness, and excited only feelings of joy and thankfulness at finding our method and aspirations crowned with so high a success. Thus was it made absolutely clear to us that, so far from divine revelation involving miracle, or requiring for its instruments persons other in kind than the ordinary, it is a prerogative of man, belonging to him as man; and requiring for its reception only that he be fully man, alive and sensitive in his own innermost and highest, in his centre as in his circumference. Thus living on the quick and finding no others who did so, it seemed to us as if we alone were the quick, and all others were dead.

We noted yet another way in which we supplemented and complemented each other. It was in this wise. As I was bent on the construction of a system of thought which should be at once a science, a philosophy, a morality, and a religion, and recognisable by the understanding as indubitably true; she was bent on the construction of a rule of life equally obvious and binding, and recognisable by the sentiments as alone according with them, its basis being that sense of perfect justice which springs from perfect sympathy.

By which it will be seen that while it was her aim to establish a perfect practice, which might or might not consist with a perfect doctrine, it was my aim to establish a perfect doctrine which would inevitably issue in a perfect practice, by at once defining it and supplying an all-compelling motive for its observance.

These, as we at once recognised, were the two indispensable halves of one perfect whole. But we had yet to learn the nature and source of the compelling motive for its enforcement.

The deficiency was made good by the discovery of the fact of man's permanence as an individual. The revelation of this truth was the demonstration to us of the inanity—not to use a stronger term—of the system called "Positivism." In ignoring the soul, that system lacks the motive and repudiates the source of the sentiments on which it insists, and to the experiences of which those sentiments are due.

CHAPTER II.
THE INITIATION.

My visit to the rectory resulted in an intimacy which made me to such extent a member of the family as to remove all obstacles to the collaboration required of us. It was soon made evident that not only our association, but her design of seeking a medical education was for both of us an indispensable element in our preparation for our now recognised joint-mission. In its general aspect that mission had for its purpose the overthrow of Materialism, and in order to qualify us for it, it was deemed necessary that we undergo a training in the most materialistic of the world's schools. This was the University of Paris. She alone was to seek a diploma. For me it was enough that I accompany her in her studies, and that we submit the teachings received by her to rigid analysis by our combined faculties. Doing this, we found ourselves competent to declare positively the falsity of the materialistic system on the strength both of logical processes and of practical demonstration, by means of the experiences of which we found ourselves the recipients. For although we had never heard of such things as "psychic faculties,"—the very phrase was not yet invented—we found ourselves possessed of them in such measure that no longer did the veil which divides the world sensible from the world spiritual constitute an impassable barrier, but both were open to view, and the latter was as real and accessible as the former.

It was about the middle of 1876 that this remarkable accession of faculty began to manifest itself in plenitude, I being the first to experience it, notwithstanding my previous total lack of any faculty of the kind, or of belief in the possibility of my having it. But the purification which my physical system had undergone by means of my new dietary regimen, and the constant and intense direction of my thought inwards and upwards, the forcible concentration of my mind upon the essential and substantial ideas of things, and this under impulsion of an enthusiasm kindled to a white heat—an enthusiasm, as already said, both of aspiration and of repulsion—and the enhancement of faculty through sympathetic association,—these had so attenuated the veil that it no longer impeded my vision of spiritual realities. And I found myself—without seeking for or expecting it—spiritually sensitive in respect of sight, hearing, and touch, and in open, palpable relations with a world which I had no difficulty in recognising as of celestial nature; so far did it transcend everything of which I had heard or read in the annals of the contemporary spiritualism; so entirely did it accord with my conceptions of the divine.

That I refrain from employing the terms "supernatural" and "superhuman," is because they assume the knowledge of the limits of the natural and the human, and arbitrarily exclude from those categories regions of being which may really belong to them. The celestial and the divine are not necessarily either superhuman or supernatural; they may be but the higher human and the higher natural. If they are at all, they are according to natural order, and it is natural for them to be.

Nevertheless, vast as was the interval it represented between my past and present states, it came so naturally and easily as to be clearly the result, not of any abnormal or accidental cataclysm involving a breach of continuity, but of a perfectly orderly unfoldment every step of which was distinctly traceable. For though the process was akin to that of the attainment of sight by one previously blind, and the final issue was sudden, the issue had been led up to in such wise as to render it legitimate and normal. For its earliest indication[18] was an opening of the mind in such wise that subjects hitherto beyond my grasp, and problems deemed insoluble, became comprehensible and clear; while whole vistas of thought perfectly continuous and coherent, would disclose themselves to my view, stretching far away towards their source in the very principles of things, so that I found myself intellectually the master of questions which previously had baffled me.

The experience I am about to relate was not only remarkable in itself, it was remarkable also as striking what proved to be the keynote of all our subsequent work, the doctrine, namely, of the *substantial* identity of God and man. It had suddenly flashed on my mind as a necessary and self-evident truth, the contrary of which was absurd; and I had seated myself at my writing-table to give it expression for a book I had lately commenced[19]. I was alone and locked in my room in my chambers off Pall Mall, Mrs Kingsford being at the time in Paris, accompanied by her husband. It was past midnight, and all without was quiet; there was not a sound to break my abstraction. This was so profound that I had written some four pages without drawing breath, the matter seeming to flow not merely from but through me without conscious mental effort of my own. I *saw* so clearly that there was no need to *think*. In the course of the writing I became distinctly aware of a presence as of someone bending over me from behind, and actively engaged in blending with and reinforcing my mind. Being unwilling to risk an interruption to the flow of my thought, I resisted the impulse to look up and ascertain who or what it was. Of alarm at so unlooked-for a presence I had not a particle. Be it whom it might, the accord between us was as perfect as if it had been merely a projection of my own higher self. I had never heard of higher selves in those days, or of the possibility of such a phenomenon; but the idea of such an explanation occurred to me then and there. But this solution of the problem of my visitant's personality was presently dissipated by the event.

The passage I had been writing concluded with these words:—

"The perfect man of any race is no other than the perfect expression in the flesh of all the essential characteristics of the soul of that race. Escaping the limitations of the individual man, such an one represents the soul of his people. Escaping the limitations of the individual people, he represents the soul of all peoples, or Humanity. Escaping the limitations of Humanity, but still preserving its essential characteristics, he represents the soul of the system of which the earth is but an individual member. And finally, after climbing many a further step of the infinite ladder of existence, and escaping the limitations of all systems whatever, he represents—nay, finds that he is—the soul of the universe, even God Himself, once 'manifested in the flesh,' and now 'perfected through suffering,' 'purified, sanctified, redeemed, justified, glorified,' 'crowned with honour and glory,' and 'seated for ever at the right hand of the Father,' 'one with God,' even God Himself."

At this moment—my mind being so wholly preoccupied with the utterance and all that I saw it involved, as to make me oblivious of all else—the presence I had felt bending over me darted itself into me just below the cerebral bulb at the back of my neck, the sensation being that of a slight tap, as of a finger-touch; and then in a voice full, rich, firm, measured, and so strong that it resounded through the room, exclaimed, in a tone indicative of high satisfaction, "At last I have found a man through whom I can speak!"

So powerful was the intonation that the tympana of my ears vibrated to the sound, palpably bulging outwards, showing that they had been struck on the inner side, and that the presence had actually projected itself into my larynx and spoken from within me, but without using my organs of speech, I was conscious of being in radiant health at the time, and was unable to detect any symptom of being otherwise. My thought, too, and observation were perfectly coherent and continuous, and I could discern no smallest pretext for distrust of the reality of the experience. And my delight and satisfaction, which were unbounded, found expression in the single utterance, "Then the ancients were right, and the Gods ARE!" so resistless was the conviction that only by a divinised being could the wisdom and power be manifested of the presence of which I was conscious. The words, "At last I have found a man" were incompatible with the theory of its being an objectivation of my own particular ego, and, moreover, they indicated the speaker as one high in authority over the race.

Nothing more passed on that occasion; but a vivid impression was left with me that my visitant belonged to the order of spirits called "Planetaries." But as I had then no knowledge of such beings, I put aside the question of his identity for the solution which I trusted would come of further enlightenment. This came in due time, with the result of confirming the impression given me at the time. The explanation, however, does not come within the scope of this present writing. Some time afterwards, when searching at the library of the British Museum in the writings of the old occultists for experiences analogous to our own, I came upon one account which described the entrance into the man of an overshadowing spirit exactly as it had occurred to me, so far as it concerned the nape of the neck as the point of entry and the slightness of the sensation. The only further reference to the incident necessary here is as follows.

A little later Mrs Kingsford had returned to England, being compelled to quit Paris by a severe illness which she had contracted immediately on her arrival there; and was pursuing her studies in London, making her home with a relative in Chelsea. The event proved that she had been sent back by the supervisors of our work expressly in order to be within reach of me. Indeed, an intimation had been given me before she had gone that she would not be allowed to stay abroad, as our near contiguity was indispensable, and I had accordingly viewed her departure with considerable disquietude, circumstances rendering it impossible for me to leave home just then. Prior to coming back she had obtained from the Minister of Education the exceptional privilege of a permit allowing her attendance at a London hospital to count in her Paris course.

The first experience received by her in relation to our work, after her return to London, was the terrific vision of "The Doomed Train"[20].

On bringing it to me on the morning of its occurrence, she exclaimed as she entered the room, "Oh, I have had such a terrific dream! It has quite shattered me. And I have brought it for you to try and find its meaning, if it has one. I wrote it down the moment I was able." Her appearance fully confirmed her statement. It alarmed me. This is the account:—

"I was visited, last night, by a dream of so strange and vivid a kind that I feel impelled to communicate it to you, not only to relieve my own mind of the oppression which the recollection of it causes me, but also to give you an opportunity of finding the meaning, which I am still far too much shaken and terrified to seek for myself.

"It seemed to me that you and I were two of a vast company of men and women, upon all of whom, with the exception of myself—for I was there voluntarily—sentence of death had been passed. I was sensible of the knowledge—how obtained I know not—that this terrible doom had been pronounced by the official agents of some new reign of terror. Certain I was that none of the party had really been guilty of any crime deserving of death; but that the penalty had been incurred through their connection with some regime, political, social, or religious, which was doomed to utter destruction. It became known among us that the sentence was about to be carried out on a colossal scale; but we remained in absolute ignorance as to the place and method of the intended execution. Thus far my dream gave me no intimation of the scene which next burst on me,—a scene which strained to their utmost tension every sense of sight, hearing, and touch in a manner unprecedented in any dream I have previously had.

"It was night, dark and starless, and I found myself, together with the whole company of doomed men and women who knew that they were soon to die, but not how or where, in a railway train hurrying through the darkness to some unknown destination. I sat in a carriage quite at the rear end of the train, in a corner seat, and was leaning out of the open window, peering into the darkness, when, suddenly, a voice, which seemed to speak out of the air, said to me in a low, distinct, intense tone, the mere recollection of which makes me shudder,—'The sentence is being carried out even now. You are all of you lost. Ahead of the train is a frightful precipice of monstrous height, and at its base beats a fathomless sea. The railway ends only with the abyss. Over that will the train hurl itself into annihilation. THERE IS NO ONE ON THE ENGINE!'

"At this I sprang from my seat in horror, and looked round at the faces of the persons in the carriage with me. No one of them had spoken, or had heard those awful words. The lamplight from the dome of the carriage flickered on the forms about me. I looked from one to the other, but saw no sign of alarm given by any of them. Then again the voice out of the air spoke to me,—'There is but one way to be saved. You must leap out of the train!'

"In frantic haste I pushed open the carriage-door and stepped out on the footboard. The train was going at a terrific pace, swaying to and fro as with the passion of its speed; and the mighty wind of its passage beat my hair about my face and tore at my garments.

"Until this moment I had not thought of you, or even seemed conscious of your presence in the train. Holding tightly on to the rail by the carriage-door, I began to creep along the footboard towards the engine, hoping to find a chance of dropping safely down on the line. Hand-over-hand I passed along in this way from one carriage to another; and as I did so I saw by the light within each carriage that the passengers had no idea of the fate upon which they were being hurried. At length, in one of the compartments, I saw *you*. 'Come out!' I cried; 'come out! Save yourself! In another minute we shall be dashed to pieces!'

"You rose instantly, wrenched open the door, and stood beside me outside on the footboard. The rapidity at which we were going was now more fearful than ever. The train rocked as it fled onwards. The wind shrieked as we were carried through it. 'Leap down!' I cried to you. 'Save yourself! It is certain death to stay here. Before us is an abyss; and there is no one on the engine!'

"At this you turned your face full upon me with a look of intense earnestness, and said, 'No, we will not leap down; we will stop the train.'

"With these words you left me, and crept along the footboard towards the front of the train. Full of half-angry anxiety at what seemed to me a Quixotic act, I followed. In one of the carriages we passed I saw my mother and eldest brother, unconscious as the rest. Presently we reached the last carriage, and saw by the lurid light of the furnace that the voice had spoken truly, and that there was no one on the engine.

"You continued to move onwards. 'Impossible! Impossible!' I cried; 'it cannot be done. Oh, pray, come away!'

"Then you knelt upon the footboard, and said, 'You are right. It cannot be done in that way; but we can save the train. Help me to get these irons asunder.'

"The engine was connected with the train by two great iron hooks and staples. By a tremendous effort, in making which I almost lost my balance, we unhooked the irons and detached the train; when, with a mighty leap as of some mad supernatural monster, the engine sped on its way alone, shooting back as it went a great flaming trail of sparks, and was lost in the darkness. We stood together on the footboard, watching in silence the gradual slackening of the speed. When at length the train had come to a standstill, we cried to the passengers, 'Saved! Saved!' And then, amid the confusion of opening the doors and descending and eager talking, my dream ended, leaving me shattered and palpitating with the horror of it."

This vision was intended to show us the destruction, moral, intellectual, and spiritual, towards which the world was tending by following materialistic modes of thought, and the part we were to bear in arresting its progress towards the fatal precipice, at all hazards to ourselves. The startling announcement made to her by the invisible voice when the crowded train was rushing at full speed to its doom, "There is no one on the engine!" exactly represented the philosophy which, denying mind in the universe, recognises only blind force.

I had determined to include an account of this vision in the book on which I was then engaged, "England and Islam." And I was alone in my rooms, reading the proofs of it, my mind being occupied solely with the letterpress, until I came to the remark ascribed to me in the vision, as made in reply to her entreaty that I would jump out with her to save ourselves, "No, we will not leap down, we will stop the train." At this moment the voice which shortly before[21] had said to me, "At last I have found a man through whom I can speak!" addressed me again, saying in a pleased and encouraging tone, as if the speaker had been following me in my reading, and desired to remove any doubts I might have of the reality of our mission,—"Yes! Yes! I have trusted all to you!" This time he spoke from without me, but apparently quite close by. And among the impressions which at the same instant were flashed into my mind, was the impression, amounting to a conviction, that whatever might be the part assigned to others in the work of the new illumination in progress and the restoration thereby to the world of one true doctrine of existence, the exposition of its innermost and highest sphere, the head corner-stone of the pyramid of the system which is to make the humanity of the future, had been committed to us alone. And now, writing nearly twenty years later, I can truly say that this conviction has never for a moment been weakened, but on the contrary has gathered confirmation and strength with every successive accession of experience and knowledge, and while cognisant of and fully appreciating all that has taken place in the unfoldment of the world's thought during the interval.

Ever since that memorable winter of 1876-7, the conviction, shared equally by my colleague, has been with me that the controlling spirit of the Hebrew prophets was that also of our work, the purpose of which was the accomplishment of their prophecies, by the promotion of the world's spiritual consciousness to a level surpassing any yet attained by it, to the regeneration of the church and the establishment of the kingdom of God with power. Having which conviction, there was for us but one object in life:—to fulfil at whatever cost to ourselves the conditions necessary to make us fitting instruments for the perfect accomplishment of a work which we recognised as the loftiest that could be committed to mortals.

My colleague's enforced return to London was promptly signalised by an experience which served not only yet further to demonstrate the reality and nature of our mission, and of her primacy in our work, but to disclose its essentially Christian character, which hitherto had been an open question for us. For that upon which we ourselves were bent was the discovery of the nature of existence at first hand, and independently of any existing system whatever. It was truth and truth alone that we sought, and to this end we had laboured to make ourselves as those of whom it is said, "Of such is the kingdom of heaven." For in divesting ourselves of all prepossessions and prejudices, we had made ourselves as "little children." We were neither believers nor disbelievers, but pure sceptics in that best sense of the term in which it denotes the unbiased seeker after God and truth. This is to say, we were, and we gloried in being, absolutely free thinkers, a term which, in its true acceptation, we regarded as man's noblest title. This is the sense in which it denotes a thought able to exercise itself in all directions open to thought, outwards and downwards to matter and negation, and inwards and upwards to spirit and reality. And our work proved in the event to be the supreme triumph of Free Thought.

The experience in question was as follows. It was night and I was alone and locked in my chambers, and was writing at full speed, lest it should escape me, an exposition of the place and office of woman under the coming regeneration. And I was conscious of an exaltation of faculty such as might conceivably be the result of an enhancement of my own mind by junction with another and superior mind. I was even conscious, though in a far less degree than before, of an invisible presence. But I was too much engrossed with my idea to pay heed to persons, be they whom they might, human or divine, as well as anxious to take advantage of such assistance. I had clearly and vividly in my mind all that I desired to say for several pages on. Then, suddenly and completely, like the stoppage of a stream in its flow through a tube by the quick turning of a tap, the current of my thought ceased, leaving my mind an utter blank as to what I had meant to say, and totally unable to recall the least idea of it. So palpable was its withdrawal, that it seemed to me as if it must still be hovering somewhere near me, and I looked up and impatiently exclaimed aloud to it, "Where are you?" At length, after ransacking my mind in vain, I turned to other work, for I was perfectly fresh, and the desertion had been in no way due to exhaustion, physical or mental. On taking note of the time of the disappearance, I found it was 11.30 precisely.

The next morning failed to bring my thought back to me as I had hoped it would do; but it brought instead, an unusually early visit from Mrs. Kingsford, who was—as I have said—staying in Chelsea. "Such a curious thing happened to me last night," she began, on entering the room, "and I want to tell you of it and see if you can explain it. I had finished my day's work, but though it was late I was not inclined to rest, for I was wakeful with a sense of irritation at the thought of what you are doing, and at my exclusion from any share in it. And I was feeling envious of your sex for the superior advantages you have over ours of doing great and useful work. As I sat by the fire thinking this, I suddenly found myself impelled to take a pencil and paper, and to write. I did so, and wrote with extreme rapidity, in a half-dreamy state, without any clear idea of what I was writing, but supposing it to be something expressive of my discontent. I had soon covered a page and a half of a large sheet with writing different from my own, and it was quite unlike what was in my mind, as you will see."

On perusing the paper I found that it was a continuation of my missing thought, taken up at the point where it had left me, but translated to a higher plane, the expression also being similarly elevated in accordance both with the theme and the writer, having the exquisiteness so characteristic of her genius. To my enquiry as to the hour of the occurrence, she at once replied, "Half-past eleven exactly; for I was so struck by it that I took particular notice of the time."

What I had written was as follows:—

"Those of us who, being men, refuse to accord to women the same freedom of evolution for their consciousness which we claim for ourselves, do so in consequence of a total misconception of the nature and functions both of Humanity and of Existence at large. The notion that men and women can by any possibility do each other's work, is utterly absurd. Whom God hath distinguished, none can confound. To do the same thing is not to do the same work; inasmuch as the spirit is more than the fact, and the spirit of man and of woman is different. While for the production of perfect results it is necessary that they work harmoniously together, it is necessary also that they fulfil separate functions in regard to that work"[22].

This was the point at which my thought had failed me, to be taken up by her at the same instant two miles away, without her knowing even that I contemplated treating that particular theme, as I had purposely reserved it until I should have completed the expression, hoping to give her a pleasant surprise; for it was one very near to her heart. This is her continuation of it. It will be seen that, besides complementing my thought, it responded remedially to her own mood:—

"In a true mission of redemption, in the proclamation of a gospel to save, it is the man who must preach; it is the man who must stand forward among the people; it is the man who, if need be, must die. But he is not alone. If his be the glory of the full noontide, his day has been ushered in by a goddess. Aurora has preceded Phoibos Apollo; Mary has been before Christ. For, mark that He shall do His first and greatest work at her suggestion. To her shall ever belong the glory of the inauguration; of her shall the gospel be born; from her lips shall the Christ take the bidding for His first miracle; from her shall His earliest inspiration be drawn. The people are athirst for the living wine, which shall be better, sweeter, purer, stronger, than any they have yet tasted. The festival lags, the joy slackens, for need of it. The Christ is in their midst, but He opens not His lips; His heart is sealed, His hour is not yet come. Mark that the first inspiration falls on the woman by His side, on Mary the Mother of God; she saith unto Him, 'They have no wine.' She has spoken, the impulse is given to Divinity. His soul awakens, His pulse quickens, He utters the word that works the miracle. Hail, Mary, full of grace; Christ is thy gift to the world! Without thee He could not have been; but for thine impulse He could have worked no mighty work. This shall be the history of all time; it shall be the sign of the Christ. Mary shall feel; Christ shall speak. Hers the glory of setting His heart in action; hers the thrill of emotion to which His power shall respond. But for her He shall be powerless; but for her He shall be dumb; but for her He shall have no strength to smite, no hand to help. It is the seed of the woman who shall bruise the serpent's head. The Christ, the true prophet, is her child, her gift to the world. 'Woman, behold thy Son!'"

Such was the first intimation and the manner thereof, given us of the truth subsequently revealed in plenitude,—the presence in Scripture of a mystical sense concealed within the apparent sense, as a kernel in its shell, which, and not the literal sense, is the intended sense[23]. As was later shown us in regard to the story of the cursing of the fig-tree, that of the marriage in Cana was a parable having a spiritual import; and the character of Jesus was cleared from the reproaches based on the literal sense. Striving for fuller unfoldment and enlightenment, we were at length enabled to discern the tremendous mistake which orthodoxy has made; the mistake of confounding, first, Jesus with Christ, and, next, Mary the mother of Jesus, with the Virgin Mary, the mother of Christ, and the conversion thereby of a perfect philosophy into a gross idolatry. Meanwhile, the experience was a further demonstration to us of the reality and accessibility not merely of the world spiritual, but of the world celestial also, and of the high source of the commission under which we had become associated together. It was also an indication that as concerned ourselves our work appertained to the spiritual, rather than to the social plane. Such application of it would follow in due time. No other hypothesis that we could devise would account for the facts. Nor could we imagine any source other than the Church invisible for an interpretation so noble of the Scriptures of the Church visible.

Not that the hypothesis of an extraneous source accounted for all our experiences. For besides receiving knowledge from such influences, there were instances in which we actually saw and seemed to remember scenes, events, and persons, long since vanished from earth, and felt at the time that it needed only that the period of lucidity be sufficiently prolonged to enable us to recover from personal recollection the whole history concerned.

I was somewhat surprised by finding the first experiences of this nature, as well as certain others of an equally high and rare order, occurring to me rather than to my colleague, of the superiority of whose faculty and of whose primacy in our work I had no manner of doubt. The explanation at length vouchsafed was in this wise. It was in order to qualify me for recognising by my own experiences the reality and value of hers when they should come. Not otherwise should I know enough to be able to believe. It proved, moreover, to be part of the plan ordained to withdraw from me, in a great measure, the faculty requisite for them, when I had become familiar with them. The reason for according her such preference over and above the superiority of her gifts will presently appear. It was another and an exquisite illustration of the depth and tenderness of the mystical element underlying Christianity as divinely conceived and intended.

The partial withdrawal from me of faculty just alluded to took place early in 1877, but not until I had undergone a thorough experiential training in its varied manifestations. Among these were two which call for relation here, by reason of their serving to show that nothing was withheld which might minister to the completeness of the work set us. The first was as follows:—

Being seated at my writing-table, and meditating on the gospel narrative, with a strange sense of being separated by only a narrow interval from a full knowledge of all that it implied, I found myself impelled to seek the precise idea intended to be conveyed by the story of the woman taken in adultery. No account that I had read of it had satisfied me, least of all that which was proposed in the "Ecce Homo" of Professor Seeley, a book then recent and enjoying a repute which filled me with a strong feeling of personal resentment. For his account, especially of the feelings excited in Jesus by the sight of the accused woman, revolted me by its inscription to Him of a sense of impropriety at once monkish and conventional, and of a limitation of charity altogether incompatible with the abounding sympathy which was the essence of His nature. It made Him that most odious of characters, a *prude*.

As I meditated, and in following my idea I passed into a state which, though highly interior, was not sufficiently interior for my purpose—for I wanted, so to speak, to *see* my idea—a voice audible only to the inner hearing, yet quite distinct, said to me, "You have it within you. Seek for it." Thus encouraged, I made a further effort at concentration, when—to my utter surprise, for I had no expectation or conception of such a thing—the whole scene of the incident appeared palpably before me, like a living picture in a *camera obscura*, so natural, minute and distinct as to leave nothing to be desired, and, at the same time, utterly unlike any pictorial representation I had ever seen of it. Close before me, on my right hand, stood the Temple, with Jesus seated on a stone ledge in the porch, while ranged before Him was a crowd of persons in the costumes of the country and the time; each costume showing the grade or calling of its wearer. Standing together in a group in front of Him were the disciples, and immediately beside them were the accusers, who were readily recognisable by their ample robes and sanctimonious demeanour; and quite close to Him, between Him and them, stood the accused woman. As I approached the scene, moving meteor-like through the air, He was in the act of lifting Himself up from stooping to write on the ground, and I had a perfect view of His face. He was of middle age, but, to my surprise, the type was that of a Murillo, rather than a Raffaelle, and the lower portion of the face was covered with a short, dark beard. The expression was worn and anxious, and somewhat weary. The skin was rough as from exposure to the weather. The eyes were deep-set and lustrous, and remarkable for the tenderness of their gaze. One of the apostles, whom I at once recognised by his comparative youthfulness as John, though his back was towards me as I approached, was in the act of bending forwards to read the words just traced in the dust on the pavement; and, as if drawn to him by some potent attraction, I at once passed unhesitatingly into him as he bent forward, and tried to read the words through his eyes. Their exact purport escaped me; but the impression I obtained was that they were unimportant in themselves, having been written merely to enable Jesus to collect and calm Himself. For He was filled with a mighty indignation, which was directed, not against the accused woman, but against the by-standing representatives of the conventional orthodoxies, the chief priests and Pharisees, her sanctimonious and hypocritical accusers,—those moral vivisectors through whose pitilessness the shrinking woman stood there exposed to the public gaze, while her fault was so brutally blurted out in her presence for all to hear; for her attitude showed her ready to sink with shame into the ground, and afraid to look either her accusers or her Judge in the face. He, her Judge, also has heard it, and knows that they who utter it are themselves a thousand-fold greater sinners than she, inasmuch as that which she has yielded through exigency either of passion or of compassion, has with them been a cold-blooded habit engendered of ingrained impurity.

In contrast with them she stands out in His eyes an angel of innocence; and an overwhelming indignation takes possession of Him, so that He will not at once trust Himself to speak. His impulse is to drive them forth with blows and reproaches from His presence, as once already He has driven the barterers from the Temple. And so, to keep His wrath from exploding, He stoops down and scribbles on the ground,—no matter what, anything to keep Himself within bounds. In the exercise His spirit calms. Indignation, He reflects, is too noble a thing to be expended upon insensates such as they, and exhortation would be vain. He will try sarcasm. So He raises himself up, and looks at them, very quietly, and even assentingly. Yes, they are quite right; the law must be vindicated, and so flagrant a sin severely punished. But, of course, only the guiltless is entitled to inflict punishment on the guilty. Therefore He says, "He of you who is blameless in respect of this sin, let him first cast a stone at her." And having said this, He stoops down again to write, this time to hide His smiles at their confusion, the sight of which would but have incensed and hardened them. What! no rush for ammunition wherewith to pound to death this only too human specimen of humanity[24]! What can be the meaning of the general move among these self-appointed censors of morals? "They which heard Him, being convicted of their own consciences, went out one by one, beginning at the eldest even unto the last." No wonder they crucified Him when they got their chance. And no wonder that most of the ancient authorities omit all mention of the incident. Even of His immediate biographers only he records it who is styled "the Beloved," and whose name, office, and character indicate him as the representative especially of the love-principle in humanity.

Such were the impressions made on me by this vision while it lasted, and written down at the time. And so strong in me was the feeling that I could similarly recall the whole history of Jesus, that I mentally addressed to the presences which I felt, though I could not see, around me an inquiry whether I should then and there begin the attempt. The reply, similarly given, was a decided negative so far as that present time was concerned, but accompanied by an intimation that our future work would comprise something of the kind; a prediction which was duly fulfilled.

I found myself perplexed beyond measure to comprehend the *modus operandi* of this experience. No explanation was forthcoming, whether from my own mind or from my illuminators, until long afterwards; and when it came it was in reference immediately to similar experiences received by my colleague, some of which likewise involved corresponding personal recollections coinciding with but surpassing mine. In the meantime the teaching given us comprised the doctrine of reincarnation, stated so positively, systematically, and scientifically that, when taken in conjunction with our experiences, we found that it, and it alone, afforded a satisfactory explanation of them. And then it was shown us that the method of the new Gospel of Interpretation, of which we were the appointed recipients, was so ordered as to be itself a demonstration of the truth of that doctrine, and that among the lives we had lived, which qualified us for our mission, were those in which we had been in association with Jesus and with each other[25]. Concerning this doctrine, the motive for its suppression, and the fatal consequences thereof to the religion of Christ, it will be time to speak when describing the results attained by us. It is with our initial experiences—those which constituted our initiation—that the present concern lies.

There is one supreme experience in the spiritual life, known to mystics as "the vision of Adonai," or God as the Lord. The reception of this vision by us was, we were assured, a conclusive proof that nothing would be withheld that was necessary to our full equipment for a complete work. Although described several times in the Bible as an actual occurrence, it had failed to find any response in our own consciousness, more than if it had no existence. Nor had it ever been the subject of intelligent comment by any Bible-expositors known to us. Rather did it seem to have been entirely passed over as a matter wholly apart from human cognition. Hence, when it was vouchsafed to us, it was entirely without anticipation of its occurrence or previous knowledge even of its possibility.

It was received first by myself, the manner of it being as follows. I had observed that when I was following an idea inwards in search of its primary meaning, and to that end concentrated my mind upon a point lying within and beyond the apparent concept, I saw a whole vista of related ideas stretching far away as if towards their source, in what I could only suppose to be the Divine Mind; and I seemed at the same time to reach a more interior region of my own consciousness; so that, supposing man's system to consist of a series of concentric spheres, each fresh effort to focus my mind upon a more recondite aspect of the idea under analysis was accompanied and marked by a corresponding advance of the perceptive point of the mind itself towards my own central sphere and radiant point. And I was prompted to try to ascertain the extent to which it was possible thus to concentrate myself interiorly, and what would be the effect of reaching the mind's ultimate focus. I was absolutely without knowledge or expectation when I yielded to the impulse to make the attempt. I simply experimented on a faculty of which I found myself newly possessed, with the view of discovering the range of its capacity, being seated at my writing-table the while in order to record the results as they came, and resolved to retain my hold on my outer and circumferential consciousness no matter how far towards my inner and central consciousness I might go. For I knew not whether I should be able to regain the former if I once quitted my hold of it, or to recollect the facts of the experience. At length I achieved my object, though only by a strong effort, the tension occasioned by the endeavour to keep both extremes of the consciousness in view at once being very great.

Once well started on my quest, I found myself traversing a succession of spheres or belts of a medium, the tenuity and luminance of which increased at every stage of my progress; the impression produced being that of mounting a vast ladder stretching from the circumference towards the centre of a system, which was at once my own system, the solar system, and the universal system, the three systems being at once diverse and identical. My progress in this ascent was clearly dependent upon my ability to concentrate the rays of my consciousness into a focus. For, while to relax the effort was to recede outwards, to intensify it was to advance inwards. The process was like that of travelling by will power from the orbit of Saturn to the Sun—taking Saturn as representing the seventh and outermost sphere of the spiritual kosmos, and the Sun its central and radiant point—with the intermediate orbits for stepping-stones and stages, I trying the while to keep both extremes in view. Presently, by a supreme, and what I felt must be a final, effort—for the tension was becoming too much for me, unless I let go my hold of the outer—I succeeded in polarising the whole of the convergent rays of my consciousness into the desired focus. And at the same instant, as if through the sudden ignition of the rays thus fused into a unity, I found myself confronted with a glory of unspeakable whiteness and brightness, and of a lustre so intense as well-nigh to beat me back. At the same instant, too, there came to me, as by a sudden recollection, the sense of being already familiar with the phenomenon, as also with its whole import, as if in virtue of having experienced it in some former and forgotten state of being. I knew it to be the "Great White Throne" of the seer of the Apocalypse. But though feeling that I had no need to explore further, I resolved to make assurance doubly sure by piercing, if I could, the almost blinding lustre, and seeing what it enshrined. With a great effort I succeeded, and the glance revealed to me that which I had felt must be there. This was the dual form of the Son, the Word, the Logos, the Adonai, the "Sitter on the Throne," the first formulation of Divinity, the unmanifest made manifest, the unformulate formulate, the unindividuate individuate, God as the Lord, proving by His Duality that God is Substance as well as Force, Love as well as Will, feminine as well as masculine, Mother as well as Father.

Overjoyed at having this supreme problem solved in accordance with my highest aspirations, my one thought was to return and proclaim the glad news. But I had no sooner set myself to write down the things thus seen and remembered, than I found myself constrained to maintain regarding them the strictest silence, and this even as regarded my fellow-worker; and all that I was permitted to say at that time was, that under a sudden burst of illumination I had become absolutely aware of the truth of the doctrine of the Duality in Unity of Deity to which that in Humanity corresponds, both alike being twain in one. On seeking the reason for the reticence thus imposed on me, I learned that the stage in our work had not yet come when it could be given to the world, either with safety to myself or with advantage to others; and it was necessary that my colleague receive no intimation in advance of any experiences which were to be given to her—of which this experience was one—in order that her mind might be wholly free from bias or expectation. Only so would our testimony have its due value as that of two independent witnesses.

In the following summer the same vision was vouchsafed to her in a measure and with a fulness far transcending mine[26].

On the occasion she had been forewarned of something of unusual solemnity as about to occur, and prompted to make certain ceremonial preparations obviously calculated to impress the imagination. The access came upon her while standing by the open window, gazing at the moon, then close upon the full. The first effect of the *afflatus* was to cause her to kneel and pray in a rapt attitude, with her arms extended towards the sky. It appeared afterwards, that under an access of spiritual exaltation, she had yielded to a sudden and uncontrollable impulse to pray that she might be taken to the stars, and shown all the glory of the universe. Presently she rose, and after gazing upwards in ecstasy for a few moments, lowered her eyes, and, clasping her arms around her head as if to shut out the view, uttered in tones of wonder, mingled with moans and cries of anguish, the following tokens of the intolerable splendour of the vision she had unwittingly invited:—

"Oh, I see masses, masses of stars! It makes me giddy to look at them. O my God, what masses! Millions and millions! WHEELS of planets! O my God, my God, why didst Thou create? It was by Will, all Will, that Thou didst it. Oh! what might, what might of Will! Oh, what gulfs! what gulfs! Millions and millions of miles broad and deep! Hold me! hold me up! I shall sink—I shall sink into the gulfs. I am sick and giddy, as on a billowy sea. I am on a sea, an ocean—the ocean of infinite space. Oh, what depths! what depths! I sink—I fail! I cannot, cannot bear it!"

"I shall never come back. I have left my body for ever. I am dying; I believe I am dead. Impossible to return from such a distance! Oh, what colossal forms! They are the angels of the planets. Every planet has its angel standing erect above it. And what beauty!—what marvellous beauty! I see Raphael. I see the Angel of the Earth. He has six wings. He is a God—the God of our planet. I see my genius, who called himself A.Z.; but his name is Salathiel. Oh, how surpassingly beautiful he is! My genius is a male, and his colour is ruby. Yours, Caro, is a female, and sapphire. They are friends—they are the same—not two, but one; and for that reason they have associated us together, and speak of themselves sometimes as *I*, sometimes as *We*. It is the Angel of the Earth himself that is your genius and mine, Caro. He it was who inspired you, who spoke to you. And they call me 'Bitterness.' And I see sorrow—oh, what unending sorrow do I behold! Sorrow, always sorrow, but never without love. I shall always have love. How dim is this sphere!... I am entering a brighter region now... Oh, the dazzling, dazzling brightness! Hide me, hide me from it! I cannot, cannot bear it! It is agony supreme to look upon. O God! O God! Thou art slaying me with Thy light. It is the Throne itself, the Great White Throne of God that I behold! Oh, what light! what light! It is like an emerald? a sapphire? No; a diamond! In its midst stands Deity erect, His right hand raised aloft, and from Him pours the light of light. Forth from His right hand streams the universe, projected by the omnipotent repulsion of His will. Back to His left, which is depressed and set backwards, returns the universe, drawn by the attraction of His love. Repulsion and attraction, will and love, right and left, these are the forces, centrifugal and centripetal, male and female, whereby God creates and redeems. Adonai! O Adonai! Lord God of life, made of the substance of light, how beautiful art Thou in Thine everlasting youth! with Thy glowing golden locks, how adorable! And I had thought of God as elderly and venerable! As if the Eternal could grow old! And now not as Man only do I behold Thee! For now Thou art to me as Woman. Lo, Thou art both. One, and Two also. And thereby dost Thou produce creation. O God, O God! why didst Thou create this stupendous existence? Surely, surely, it had been better in love to have restrained Thy will. It was by will that Thou createdst, by will alone, not by love, was it not?—was it not? I cannot see clearly. A cloud has come between.

"I see Thee now as Woman. Maria is next beside Thee. Thou art Maria. Maria is God. Oh Maria! God as Woman! Thee, thee I adore! Maria-Aphrodite! Mother! Mother-God!

"They are returning with me now, I think. But I shall never get back. What strange forms! how huge they are! All angels and archangels. Human in form, yet some with eagles' heads. All the planets are inhabited! how innumerable is the variety of forms! Oh! universe of existence, how stupendous is existence! Oh! take me not near the sun; I cannot bear its heat. Already do I feel myself burning. Here is Jupiter! It has nine moons! Yes; nine. Some are exceedingly small. And, oh, how red it is! It has so much iron. And what enormous men and women! There is evil there, too. For evil is wherever are matter and limitation. But the people of Jupiter are far better than we on earth. They know much more; they are much wiser. There is less evil in their planet. Ah! and they have another sense, too. What is it? No; I cannot describe it. I cannot tell what it is. It differs from any of the others. We have nothing like it. I cannot get back yet. I shall never get back. I believe I am dead. It is only my body you are holding. It has grown cold for want of me. Yet I must be approaching; it is growing shallower. We are passing out of the depths. Yet I can never wholly return—never—never!"[27]

The account given of the vision of Adonai in Lecture IX. of "The Perfect Way," was written solely from our joint experiences. It was with an interest altogether novel in kind and degree that I now turned to the Bible narratives of the same vision, and found that in the record of its reception by the Elders of Israel, it is stated, as if in token of the power of the spiritual battery with which Moses had surrounded himself, that no less than seventy of his initiates were able to receive the vision without magnetic reinforcement by the imposition of their master's hands. But, as we learnt from our own manifold experiences, it does not follow that because there is no imposition of visible hands, no extraneous aid is rendered. The seeker after God cannot, even if he would, accomplish his quest alone; but always are there attracted to him those angelic beings whose office it is, as ministers of God, to sustain and illuminate souls by the imposition of hands invisible to the outer senses. In her case such aid was palpable. There was no effort on her part. And she held converse with those by whom she was upborne in her stupendous flight.

When in due course the time came for us to receive the ancient and long-lost Gnosis which underlay the sacred religions and scriptures of antiquity, the following was given us, and we recognised in it the original Scripture from which the opening sentences in St John's Gospel are drawn.

After defining the Elohim as comprising the two original principles of all Being, "the Spirit and the Water," or Force and Substance, and bringing up the process whereby Deity proceeds into manifestation to the point described in Genesis in the words, "And the Spirit of God moved upon the face of the Waters. And God *said*,"—the utterance thus continues,—

Then from the midst of the Divine Duality, the Only Begotten of God came forth:

Adonai, the Word, the Voice invisible.

He was in the beginning, and by Him were all things discovered.

Without Him was not anything made which is visible.

For He is the Manifestor, and in Him was the life of the world.

God the nameless hath not revealed God, but Adonai hath revealed God from the beginning.

He is the presentation of Elohim, and by Him the Gods are made manifest.

He is the third aspect of the Divine Triad:

Co-equal with the Spirit and the heavenly deep.

For except by three in one, the Spirits of the Invisible Light could not have been made manifest.

But now is the prism perfect, and the generation of the Gods discovered in their order.

Adonai dissolves and resumes; in His two hands are the dual powers of all things.

He is of His Father the Spirit, and of His Mother the great deep.

Having the potency of both in Himself, and the power of things material.

Yet being Himself invisible, for He is the cause, and not the effect.

He is the Manifestor, and not that which is manifest.

That which is manifest is the Divine Substance[28].

The reason for the suppression by the translators of the Bible of its numerous affirmations of the Divine Duality, saving only those of Genesis i. 26, 27, was in due time disclosed to us; as also was the extent of the loss to man through the elimination of the feminine principle from his conception of Original Being, and the consequent perversion of the doctrine of the Trinity, and therein of the true nature of Existence, in both its aspects, Creation and Redemption.

CHAPTER III.
THE COMMUNICATION.

A striking feature for us was the exquisite tenderness and poetic delicacy, both in matter and manner, which characterised all that we received. Nor was there the intrusion of anything to suggest feelings such as are described by Daniel when he says, "I saw this great vision, and there remained no strength in me, neither was there breath left in me." And not only was the element of terror so completely absent as to make us feel as if we had entered on the dispensation of that "perfect love which casteth out fear," but there was occasionally an element of playfulness, and this on the part of our chiefest illuminators, the Gods themselves. While their instructions were replete with every graceful and delicate adornment such as could not but delight the poet and the artist, and this without abatement of profundity or solemnity. By these things it was intimated to us that the religion of the future was indeed to be one of sweetness and light, and for the severe and gloomy spirit of the Semite would be substituted the bright and joyous spirit of the Greek. All this, we learnt, was because the new dispensation was to be that of the "Woman," and in accord therefore with woman's nature and sentiments. It was moreover to be introduced by means of the Woman's faculty, the Intuition, and this as subsisting in *a* woman.

The following exquisite little apologue, which was given us in the early days of our novitiate, is an instance in point:—

A blind man once lost himself in a forest. An angel took pity on him, and led him into an open place. As he went he received his sight. Then he saw the angel, and said to him, "Brother, what doest thou here? Suffer me to go before thee, for I am thine elder." So the man went first, taking the lead. But the angel spread his wings and returned to heaven. And darkness fell again upon him to whom sight had been given.

Here was a parable which, slight as it seemed, was truly Biblical for the depth and manifoldness of its signification. For while it applied to ourselves both separately and jointly, and to our work, it was also an eternal verity applicable alike to the individual, the collective, and the universal. For as the angel was to the man, so is the intuition to the intellect, which of itself cannot transcend the sense-nature, but remains blind and dark and lost in the wilderness of illusion. And as she, my colleague, had supplemented me, so were we each to supplement in ourselves intellect by intuition, in order to become capable of knowledge and understanding. It was, moreover, a parable of the Fall and of the Redemption, an epitome in short of man's spiritual history. And it had been spelt out for us by the tilting of a table in one of our earliest essays in spiritualism! So carefully guarded and daintily taught were we from the outset.

The charming allegory of "The Wonderful Spectacles" which was given in London on the 31st January, 1877, to my colleague in sleep, was not only an instruction concerning the nature of her faculty and its indispensableness as an adjunct to mine for the work assigned to us; it was also a prophetic intimation of the character of that work, and of the nature of the influences controlling it, which at the time was altogether unsuspected by us. This is the account which she sent to me by letter, for we were not then together:—

I dreamt that I was walking alone on the sea-shore. The day was singularly clear and sunny. Inland lay the most beautiful landscape ever seen; and far off were ranges of tall hills, the highest peaks of which were white with glistening snow. Along the sands by the sea towards me came a man accoutred as a postman. He gave me a letter. It was from you. It ran thus:—

"I have got hold of the rarest and most precious book extant. It was written before the world began. The text is easy enough to read; but the notes, which are very copious and numerous, are in such very minute and obscure characters that I cannot make them out. I want you to get for me the spectacles which Swedenborg used to wear; not the smaller pair—those he gave to Hans Christian Andersen—but the large pair, and these seem to have got mislaid. I think they are Spinoza's make. You know he was an optical-glass maker by profession, and the best we have ever had. See if you can get them for me"[29].

When I looked up after reading this letter, I saw the postman hastening away across the sands, and I called out to him, "Stop! how am I to send the answer? Won't you wait for me?"

He looked round, stopped, and came back to me.

"I have the answer here," he said, tapping his letter bag, "and I shall deliver it immediately."

"How can you have the answer before I have written it?" said I. "You are making a mistake."

"No," said he, "In the city from which I come, the replies are all written at the office and sent out with the letters themselves. Your reply is in my bag."

"Let me see it," I said. He took another letter from his wallet and gave it to me. I opened it, and read, in my own handwriting, this answer, addressed to you:—

"The spectacles you want can be bought in London. But you will not be able to use them at once, for they have not been worn for many years, and they want cleaning sadly. This you will not be able to do yourself in London, because it is too dark there to see, and because your fingers are not small enough to clean them properly. Bring them here to me, and I will do it for you."

I gave this letter back to the postman. He smiled and nodded at me; and I saw then to my astonishment that he wore a camel's-hair tunic round his waist. I had been on the point of addressing him—I know not why—as *Hermes*. But I now saw that it was John the Baptist; and in my fright at having spoken with so great a saint, I awoke.

This was the second suggestion of a Greek element in our work, the first having been the slight allusion to Phoibos Apollo in the illumination concerning the Marriage in Cana of Galilee[30]. The signification of the connection between Hermes and John the Baptist remained unintelligible to us until the key to it was given us in a revelation of the method of the Bible-writers explaining their practice of representing principles as persons. We then found that by the baptism or purification, physical and mental, practised by John, was meant the course of life and thought whereby alone man develops the faculty of the understanding of spiritual things. And Hermes is the Greco-Egyptian name for the "second of the Gods," called by Isaiah the Spirit of Understanding. Hence the adoption of this name by the formulators of the Hermetic, or sacred books of Egypt; and the favourite motto of the Hermetists:—

"Est in Mercurio quicquid quœrunt sapientes,"

All is in the understanding that the wise seek,—Mercury being the Latin equivalent for Hermes.

The mention of Swedenborg and Andersen implied their possession of the faculty indispensable to our work, that of mystical insight, of which they were the most notable recent representatives.

A larger part was played by Hermes in another instruction received a few months later[31]. This was also given in sleep, the vision taking the form of a "Banquet of the Gods" in which the seeress received the following exhortation from him, in enforcement of the necessity of pure and natural habits of life for the perfectionment of the faculties requisite for full spiritual perception, when, having put into her hands a branch of a fig-tree bearing upon it ripe fruit, he said:—

"If you would be perfect, and able to know and to do all things, quit the heresy of Prometheus. Let fire warm and comfort you externally: it is heaven's gift. But do not wrest it from its rightful purpose, as did that betrayer of your race, to fill the veins of humanity with its contagion, and to consume your interior being with its breath. All of you are men of clay, as was the image which Prometheus made. Ye are nourished with stolen fire, and it consumes you. Of all the evil uses of heaven's good gifts, none is so evil as the internal use of fire. For your hot foods and drinks have consumed and dried up the magnetic power of your nerves, sealed your senses, and cut short your lives. Now, you neither see nor hear; for the fire in your organs consumes your senses. Ye are all blind and deaf, creatures of clay. We have sent you a book to read. Practise its precepts, and your senses shall be opened."

Then, not recognising him, I said, "Tell me your name, Lord." At this he laughed and answered, "I have been about you from the beginning. I am the white cloud on the noon-day sky." "Do you, then," I asked, "desire the whole world to abandon the use of fire in preparing food and drink?"

Instead of answering my question, he said, "We show you the excellent way. Two places only are vacant at our table. We have told you all that can be shown you on the level on which you stand. But our perfect gifts, the fruits of the Tree of Life, are beyond your reach now. We cannot give them to you until you are purified and have come up higher. The conditions are GOD'S; the will is with you"[32].

The allusion to Prometheus, and the fact that Hermes had been represented in the Greek tragedy of that name as the executor of the vengeance of the Gods upon Prometheus, as well also as the significance of the fig-branch and the fact of its being the symbol of Hermes as the Spirit of Understanding,—all these things were beyond her knowledge at the time, some of them indeed having been long lost. But all were made clear as our education for our work proceeded, and we learnt the intention and recognised the necessity of restoring the Greek presentment of the Sacred Mysteries in explanation of the Hebrew, and in correction of the ecclesiastical presentment of Christianity. The restoration was to be twofold, of faculty and of knowledge, the knowledge to be recovered through the faculty by which it was originally obtained. Hence the insistance on our adoption of the pure regimen of the Seers of all time. Hence, too, the presentation to her by Hermes of the fig-branch bearing ripe fruit. The parable of the cursing of the barren fig-tree was explained to us as denoting the loss by the church of the inward understanding, the

Intuition. In the Seeress it was restored; she was the appointed representative of it. The "time of the end" was at hand, of the approach of which the budding of the fig-tree was to be the sign. And here it was not merely budding and blossoming, but bearing mature fruit to signify that in her the faculty was restored in its perfection.

In an instruction subsequently given to me by her Genius, he said of her, "I have fashioned a perfect instrument," implying that the process of her preparation under his tuition had extended over numerous lives. And again, "The Gods have given to their own a perfect ear."

Being desirous once to test the powers of a medium to whom she was totally unknown even by name, she asked his controlling spirit about herself and her faculty. "You are not a trance-medium at all!" the spirit exclaimed in reply. "My medium is a trance-medium. You are far beyond that. You are a spiritual lens. You are a mirror in which the highest spirits—the Gods—can reflect their faces. You take the light of the whole universe and divide it so that it can be understood, as it has never been understood yet. Your gift is very extraordinary. You are a glass to reflect the highest and the greatest to the world." This was in 1877, before she was known in connection with the spiritual movement of the age.

The description given of himself by Hermes as "the white cloud in the noon-day sky," proved to be a quotation from an ancient ritual, subsequently recovered by her, in which the "Hymn to Hermes"[33] opens thus:—

As a moving light between heaven and earth: as a white cloud assuming many shapes;

He descends and rises: he guides and illumines; he transmutes himself from small to great, from bright to shadowy, from the opaque image to the diaphanous mist.

Star of the East, conducting the Magi; cloud from whose midst the holy voice speaketh; by day a pillar of vapour, by night a shining flame.

All these are symbolic expressions for the Understanding, especially in respect of divine things, so that Hermes is no individual soul or spirit, but the divine spirit Itself operating as the second of the Creative Elohim, and as a function therefore of man's own spirit when duly unfolded and purified, in token whereof it is said in the recovered hymn[34] to the Planet-God Iacchos—

Within thee, O Man, is the Universe; the thrones of all the Gods are in thy temple....

And the Spirits which speak unto thee are of thine own kingdom.

In the hymn of invocation summoning the Seeress to her mission in the name of the two first of the "Holy Seven," the Spirits of Wisdom and Understanding, both of whom were wont to manifest themselves to her, Hermes is referred to as "the God who knows"; the other being personified as Pallas Athena. "In the Celestial," we were informed, "all things are Persons."

"Wake, prophet-soul, the time draws near,
'The God who knows' within thee stirs
And speaks, for His thou art, and Hers
Who bears the mystic shield and spear.

A touch divine shall thrill thy brain,
Thy soul shall leap to life, and lo!
What she has known, again shall know,
What she has seen, shall see again.

The ancient past through which she came..." [35]

As the Spirit of Understanding, the name of Hermes signifies both Rock and Interpreter. Hence the significance of the saying of Jesus, "Thou art the Rock, and upon this Rock I will build My Church," which He addressed not to the man Peter, but to the Spirit of Understanding whom He discerned as the prompter of Peter's confession of faith. By this Jesus implied that the only true and infallible church is that which is founded on the Understanding, and not on authority whether of book, tradition or institution. The utterance of Jesus was a citation from the proem to the hymn to Hermes[36] recovered by us:—

"He is as a rock between earth and heaven, and the Lord God shall build His Church thereon.

As a city upon a mountain of stone, whose windows look forth on either side."

As our education proceeded we found indubitably that in excluding from its curriculum the whole range of the knowledges represented by the term "Hermetic," Ecclesiasticism has ignored the chief source of information concerning the Christian *origines*. Doing which it has incurred the reproach uttered by Jesus against those who took away the key of knowledge, neither entering in themselves, nor suffering others to enter in. And it was to restore this Gnosis, suppressed by the priests, that the new revelation was promised, with the reception of which we found ourselves charged, the prophecies pointing to a restoration both of faculty and of knowledge.

Besides the Fig-branch of Hermes, there is another symbol of the intuitional understanding which was disclosed to us as having special and peculiar relation to the work set us. This symbol is Woman herself. She had already, in the instruction concerning the marriage in Cana[37], been shown to us as the inspirer and prompter. She was now shown to us as the interpreter. The reason why the fig-tree was the emblem of the inward understanding will be found in the citation presently to be given; which is a portion of an instruction received in interpretation of the prophecy of Daniel, re-enunciated by Jesus, concerning the recognition of the "abomination of desolation standing in the holy place"[38], as making and marking the time of the end of that generation which, for its materialisation of spiritual things, was called by Him an "adulterous," meaning an idolatrous, generation. It will be seen that in the Scripture symbology, as the soul is the feminine principle in man's spiritual system, and is called therefore the "Woman," the spirit being the masculine principle; so in man's mental system the intuition as the feminine mode of the mind is called the "Woman," and the intellect, as the masculine mode, the "Man." The following is the citation in question:—

Behold the FIG-TREE, and learn her parable. When the branch thereof shall become tender, and her buds appear, know that the day of God is upon you.

Wherefore, then, saith the Lord that the budding of the Fig-Tree shall foretell the end?

Because the Fig-Tree is the symbol of the Divine Woman, as the Vine of the Divine Man.

The Fig is the similitude of the Matrix, containing inward buds, bearing blossoms on its placenta, and bringing forth fruit in darkness. It is the Cup of Life, and its flesh is the seed-ground of new births.

The stems of the Fig-Tree run with milk: her leaves are as human hands, like the leaves of her brother the Vine.

And when the Fig-Tree shall bear figs, then shall be the Second Advent, the new sign of the Man bearing Water, and the manifestation of the Virgin-Mother crowned.

For when the Lord would enter the holy city, to celebrate His Last Supper with His disciples, He sent before Him the Fisherman Peter to meet the Man of the Coming Sign.

"There shall meet you a Man bearing a pitcher of Water."

Because, as the Lord was first manifest at a wine-feast in the morning, so must He consummate His work at a wine-feast in the evening.

It is His Pass-Over; for thereafter the Sun must pass into a new Sign.

After the Fish, the Water-Carrier; but the Lamb of God remains always in the place of victory, being slain from the foundation of the world.

For His place is the place of the Sun's triumph.

After the Vine the Fig; for Adam is first formed, then Eve.

And because our Lady is not yet manifest, our Lord is crucified.

Therefore came He vainly seeking fruit upon the Fig-Tree, "for the time of figs was not yet."

And from that day forth, because of the curse of Eve, no man has eaten fruit of the Fig-Tree.

For the inward understanding has withered away, there is no discernment any more in men. They have crucified the Lord because of their ignorance, not knowing what they did.

Wherefore, indeed, said our Lord to our Lady:—"Woman, what is between me and thee? For even *my* hour is not yet come."

Because until the hour of the Man is accomplished and fulfilled, the hour of the Woman must be deferred.

Jesus is the Vine; Mary is the Fig-Tree. And the vintage must be completed and the wine trodden out, or ever the harvest of the Figs be gathered.

But when the hour of our Lord is achieved; hanging on His Cross, He gives our Lady to the faithful.

The chalice is drained, the lees are wrung out: then says He to His Elect:— "Behold thy Mother!"

But so long as the grapes remain unplucked, the Vine has nought to do with the Fig-Tree, nor Jesus with Mary.

He is first revealed, for He is the Word; afterwards shall come the hour of its Interpretation.

And in that day every man shall sit under the VINE and the FIG-TREE; the Dayspring shall arise in the Orient, and the Fig-Tree shall bear her fruit.

For, from the beginning, the Fig-leaf covered the shame of Incarnation, because the riddle of existence can be expounded only by him who has the Woman's secret. It is the riddle of the Sphinx.

Look for that Tree which alone of all Trees bears a fruit blossoming interiorly, in concealment, and thou shalt discover the Fig.

Look for the sufficient meaning of the manifest universe and of the written Word, and thou shalt find only their mystical sense.

Cover the nakedness of Matter and of Nature with the Fig-leaf, and thou hast hidden all their shame. For the Fig is the Interpreter.

So when the hour of Interpretation comes, and the Fig-Tree puts forth her buds, know that the time of the End and the dawning of the new Day are at hand,—"even at the doors."

On handing me the first portion of the instruction of which the foregoing is the conclusion, "Mary"—to use the name which meanwhile had been bestowed on her by our Illuminators in token of her office as representative of the Soul and Intuition—confessed to some perplexity. Her usual Illuminator for revelations of this order was Hermes, whose Hebrew equivalent is Raphael. But on this occasion it had been a Hebrew one, Gabriel. Her surprise and delight were great on being reminded that Gabriel was Daniel's own inspirer in respect of the prophecy in question, and that he had prophesied his return, saying, "Go thy way, Daniel, for the words are closed up and sealed till the time of the end.... Thou shalt rest and stand in thy lot at the end of the days." The explanation given us was that both Daniel's own spirit and his illuminating angel had come to her, the former serving as the vehicle of the latter. As with all our other results similarly obtained, we judged it entirely by its own intrinsic merits, and not by its alleged derivation. We knew too well the propensity of low influences to appropriate to themselves great and even divine names, and the liability of the recipients to be deceived and to make the names the criterion instead of the communication itself. But in no instance did it happen to us that we had any cause to distrust the genuineness either of messenger or of message, even when both claimed to be divine.

The difference between the two interpretations or applications given us of the incident at the "Marriage in Cana of Galilee," was explained to us as an instance of the manifoldness of the sense of Scripture. The parables have a separate meaning for each of the four planes of existence[39].

We wondered much whether there were any parallels in history to our work and to the manner of it; and especially as to how far an association such as ours coincided with the ideas of the Hebrews. It was true that they had both prophets and prophetesses, but did they work like us in supplement and complement of each other? As regarded the recovery of knowledge acquired in a previous life, Ezra also had ascribed his recovery of the long lost Law to intuitional recollection occurring under special illumination, saying, "The Spirit strengthened my memory." But no mention is made of a female coadjutor. Nor does it appear that the Vestal Virgins were similarly supplemented, except to be thrown into the magnetic trance-state. In her zeal for her sex and her corresponding distrust of men—sentiments which seemed to be inborn in her—"Mary" was disposed to think that most of the prophesying of old had been done by women, but that the credit had been appropriated by men. The answer to these questionings was of a kind altogether unexpected by us, both as regarded its manner and its matter. For neither of us had the smallest suspicion that the book referred to was capable of the interpretation given us of it. This was the book of Esther. The incident was as follows:—

The occasion was an Easter Sunday[40], and we were at Paris. Electing to remain indoors rather than encounter the crowds of holiday makers, "Mary" was moved during the afternoon to sit for some communication by joint writing. But we were no sooner seated than it was written,—

"Do you, Caro[41], take a pencil and write, and let her look inwards, and we will dictate slowly."

"Mary" then became entranced, and delivered orally, repeating it slowly, without break or pause, after a voice heard interiorly, the following exposition of the book of Esther, an exposition entirely novel, as I have said, to us, and, we believed, to the world. Some divines have called the book a romance, but none have discovered that it is a prophecy in the form of a parable. Luther, indeed, pronounced both it and the Apocalypse to be so worthless that their destruction would be no loss.

The most important book in the Bible for you to study now, and that most nearly about to be fulfilled, is one of the most mystic books in the Old Testament, the book of Esther.

This book is a mystic prophecy, written in the form of an actual history. If I give you the key, the clue of the thread of it, it will be the easiest thing in the world to unravel the whole.

The great King Assuerus, who had all the world under his dominion, and possessed the wealth of all the nations, is the genius of the age.

Queen Vasthi, who for her disobedience to the king was deposed from her royal seat, is the orthodox Catholic Church.

The Jews, scattered among the nations under the dominion of the king, are the true Israel of God.

Mardochi the Jew represents the spirit of intuitive reason and understanding.

His enemy Aman is the spirit of materialism, taken into the favour and protection of the genius of the age, and exalted to the highest place in the world's councils after the deposition of the orthodox religion.

Now Aman has a wife and ten sons.

Esther—who, under the care and tuition of Mardochi, is brought up pure and virgin—is that spirit of love and sympathetic interpretation which shall redeem the world.

I have told you that it shall be redeemed by a "woman."

Now the several philosophical systems by which the councillors of the age propose to replace the dethroned Church, are one by one submitted to the judgment of the age; and Esther, coming last, shall find favour.

Six years shall she be anointed with oil of myrrh, that is, with study and training severe and bitter, that she may be proficient in intellectual knowledge, as must all systems which seek the favour of the age.

And six years with sweet perfumes, that is with the gracious loveliness of the imagery and poetry of the faiths of the past, that religion may not be lacking in sweetness and beauty.

But she shall not seek to put on any of those adornments of dogma, or of mere sense, which, by trick of priestcraft, former systems have used to gain power or favour with the world and the age, and for which they have been found wanting.

Now there come out of the darkness and the storm which shall arise upon the earth, two dragons[42].

And they fight and tear each other, until there arises a star, a fountain of light, a queen, who is Esther[43].

I have given you the key. Unlock the meaning of all that is written.

I do not tell you if in the history of the past these voices had part in the world of men.

If they had, guess now who were Mardochi and Esther.

But I tell you that which shall be in the days about to come[44].

On consulting the Bible-dictionary, we found this relation between Esther and Easter. The feast of Purim, which was instituted in token of the deliverance wrought through Esther, coincides in date with Easter. And it was on Easter day that this was given us, by way of enhancing the correspondence between the parts assigned to us and those of Mordecai and Esther. Later it was shown us that the parts assigned to Joseph and Mary were, in one aspect, also identical with those of Mordecai and Esther. This is the aspect in which Joseph represents the mind, and Mary the soul in the regenerated human system.

Besides "Hermes," "Mary" received much of her illumination from her "Genius," her relations with whom far surpassed not only my relations with mine, but any that are recorded in history, the experiences of Socrates, the chief instance on record, being insignificant both in quantity and in quality as compared with hers. It is important, therefore, to give an account of the nature and office of this order of angels, which shall be rendered in his own words.

Every man is a planet, having sun, moon, and stars. The Genius of a man is his satellite; God—the God of the man—is his sun, and the moon of this planet is Isis, its initiator or Genius. The Genius is made to minister to the man, and to give him light. But the light he gives is from God, and not of himself. He is not a planet but a moon, and his function is to light up the dark places of his planet.

The day and night of the microcosm, man, are its positive and passive, or protective and reflective states. In the projective state we seek actively outwards; we aspire and will forcibly; we hold active communion with the God without. In the reflective state we look inwards; we commune with our own heart; we indraw and concentrate ourselves secretly and interiorly. During this condition the "Moon" enlightens our hidden chamber with her torch, and shows us ourselves in our interior recess.

Who or what, then, is this moon? It is part of ourselves and revolves with us. It is our celestial affinity,—of whose order it is said—as by Jesus—"Their angels do always behold the face of My Father."

Every human soul has a celestial affinity, which is part of his system and a type of his spiritual nature. This angelic counterpart is the bond of union between the man and God; and it is in virtue of his spiritual nature that this angel is attached to him....

It is in virtue of man's being a planet that he has a moon. If he were not fourfold, as is the planet, he could not have one. Rudimentary men are not fourfold, they have not the Spirit.

The Genius is the moon to the planet man, reflecting to him the Sun, or God, within him. For the Divine Spirit which animates and eternises the man, is the God of the man, the Sun that enlightens him.... And because the Genius reflects, not the planet, but the Sun, not the man (as do the astrals), but the God, his light is always to be trusted....

The memory of the soul is recovered by a threefold operation—that of the Soul herself, of the Moon, and of the Sun. The Genius is not an informing spirit. He can tell nothing to the soul. All that she receives is already within herself. But in the darkness of the night, it would remain there undiscovered, but for the torch of the angel who enlightens. "Yea," says the angel Genius to his client, "I illuminate thee, but I instruct thee not. I warn thee, but I fight not. I attend, but I lead not. Thy treasure is within thyself. My light showeth where it lieth."...

The voice of the Genius is the voice of God; for God speaks through him as a man through the horn of a trumpet. Thou mayest not adore him, for he is the instrument of God, and thy minister. But thou must obey him, for he hath no voice of his own, but sheweth thee the will of the Spirit.

We noted that the inspiring angel of the Apocalypse had twice similarly spoken when the seer was about to worship him;—"See thou do it not; for I am thy fellow-servant, and of thy brethren the prophets, and of them which keep the sayings of this book: Worship God."

The like positive injunctions were given us also against according divine honours to Jesus.

Besides Socrates, there is another notable historical "Spiritualist" of whom our experiences vividly reminded us. This was Joan of Arc. The correspondence between her and "Mary," in gifts, experiences, and personal characteristics, was of the closest. We had no difficulty in believing her history. Each of them, moreover, had a mission of deliverance, the one political and national, the other spiritual and universal.

Although we had learned to trust our Illuminators implicitly long before the receipt of the above instruction, we were still without assurance as to the source and method of the revelation. Be the knowledges received by us as new as they might to our external selves, they never failed to be familiar as recovered memories, excepting in such cases as they were couched in terms of which the sense, being mystical, was not at once recognised. But such difficulties were soon overcome, and the doctrine, when fully apprehended, was always to us as necessary and self-evident truth, and such as to excite wonder at the potency of the glamour which had hitherto withheld it from the world's recognition. In every detail, the revelation represented for us Common-Sense in its loftiest mode. For the agreement it represented was not that of all men merely, but that of all parts of Man: of mind, soul and spirit, intellect and intuition, and these purified and unfolded to the utmost, and perfectly equilibrated. Whatever the manner of its communication, whether heard by the interior ear, seen by the interior eye, flashed on the mind as vivid ideas, whether acquired waking or sleeping, or in the intermediate state of trance-lucidity, or given in writing, it always seemed that we knew it before, and did not require to be told it, but only to be reminded of it.

The problem specially exercised myself. "Mary" had other work than the analysis of our spiritual experiences. That was my special function. I learnt to see in her a soul of surpassing luminousness and variousness, who had been entrusted to my charge expressly in order that by my study of her I might recover for the world's benefit the long-lost knowledge of the soul's being, nature, and history. And so many and various were her spiritual states, that she seemed to me to represent in turn every stage of the soul's evolution, and to be "not one, but all mankind's epitome."

This also used to occur so frequently as to be observed by both of us and discussed between us. When in the process of my endeavour to find the solution of some problem, such as the meaning of a parabolic or otherwise obscure passage in Scripture, I had exhausted my stock of tentative hypotheses, but, through consideration for her other and engrossing work, refrained from imparting my need to her, she would receive in sleep the desired solution, which she wrote down on waking, and which invariably proved satisfactory beyond my highest imaginings. And besides showing intimate acquaintance with the course of my thought, it was couched in language which, for simplicity, dignity, purity, and lucidity, was without an equal in literature; the English being that of the best period of our literature, and better than the best even of that period. She herself had a remarkable mastery of English, but these compositions reduced her to despair, causing her to exclaim, "Why cannot I write as well when I am awake as I do in my sleep!" Of course the explanation lay in the limiting influence of the physical organism.

The frequency of this occurrence led me, in the absence of authoritative explanation, to try the following, as an hypothesis purely tentative. The revelations generally came to her when, through my inability to find the interpretations which satisfied me, my work required them, and they came independently of any desire or knowledge on her part. Might it not be, then, that it was my own spirit who knew them and gave them to her, finding her more sensitive to impression than myself? The explanation was not one that either pleased or satisfied me, one reason being that I took a delight in recognising the primacy accorded to her. The idea occurred to me one night, and I pondered it the next day, but did not divulge it. What happened on the evening of that day led me to suspect that our Genii had suggested it to me in order to make it the occasion of imparting to me the knowledge in question, namely, that of the real source and method of the revelation.

For the experience to be properly appreciated it must be remembered that "Mary" had no knowledge of the explanation suggested to me, and neither of us had as yet entertained the idea of past lives as the key to our present work. The question of Reincarnation itself had not come before us, and far less the possibility of recovering the memory of the things learnt in previous existences, much as we had been puzzled to account for our experiences in the absence of some such explanation.

The proposal to sit for a written communication came from her, having evidently been prompted by our illuminators. The method was one which both they and we disliked, and it was adopted only when they desired to address us both at once. So we sat for writing.

The result confirmed my surmise. We had scarcely seated ourselves when the writing began, as if we were being waited for. And this is what was written:—

"We are instructed to say several things to-night. We are your Genii.

"(To CARO.) In the first place, you entirely misconceive the process by which the Revelation comes to Mary. The method of this revelation is entirely interior. Mary is not a Medium; nor is she even a Seer as you understand the word. She is a Prophet. By this we mean that all she has ever written or will write, is from within, and not from without. She knows. She is not told. Hers is an old, old spirit. She is older than you are, Caro, older by many thousand years. Do not think that spirits other than her own are to be credited with the authorship of the new Gospel. As a proof of this, and to correct the false impression you have on the subject, the holy and inner truth, of which she is the depositary, will not in future be given to her by the former method. All she writes henceforth, she will write consciously. Yes, she must finish the new Evangel by conscious effort of brain and will."

Coming from a source which we had learnt to trust implicitly, and according with our own highest conceptions, this message was supremely satisfactory, and was welcomed accordingly. But it was followed forthwith by another which excited feelings of a very different character. For, as if expressly in order to prevent her from being made vain-glorious and uplifted by it, they added—

"(To MARY.) It may serve to exhibit the path by which you have come, and to suggest the nature of some ancient tendencies which may yet tarnish the mirror of a soul destined to attain perfection, to learn that you dwelt within the body of———."

Here were given the name and character of a certain Roman dame of some seventeen centuries ago, one of high station, but of a repute so evil as to cause an immense shock to both of us. It does not come within the design of this book to disclose the particular personalities with whom we had been identified in the past[45]. Concerning this one it must suffice to state here that, omitting from account one whole side of "Mary's" character, we both recognised in the other side traits strongly resembling those which had been indicated. And she subsequently recovered distinct recollections of scenes in the life in question which served to assure her on the point. Our discussions on the matter tended to conclusions of which fuller knowledge brought the verification. It was not one of those lives in virtue of which she was directly qualified for her present work; but it was one of those lives of which the sin and the suffering may well be conceived of as indispensable elements in the education of a soul called to a lofty work and destiny in the future, in accordance with the principle which finds expression in the sayings, "The greater the sinner the greater the saint," and "*Pecca Fortiter.*" This also we discerned clearly, that, supposing it to be indeed a truth that man is "made perfect through suffering," the experiences in the course of which the suffering is undergone must imply sin as well as pain and sorrow; since otherwise there would be a whole region of his nature, namely the moral, in which he would remain unvitalised. The lesson of which is that a man is alive only so far as he has lived. There was yet another reflection that was prompted by the occasion in question, and one which crowned and glorified the rest. This was the assurance implied that none need despair. If the soul which had dwelt in the body of the person named, could nevertheless become within measureable time what "Mary" was now, and be "destined to attain perfection," there is hope for all, and the doctrine of Reincarnation is indeed a gospel of salvation. And herein we discerned a lesson hitherto unsuspected so far as we were aware, in the parable of the Prodigal Son. It is not the "elder brother" who stays at home that can best appreciate the divine order; but the prodigal who has gone forth into the world of experience to acquire knowledge for himself at first hand. They who have been the most fully satiated with the husks of materiality, can—when their time arrives for coming to their true selves—best estimate the fare provided in the "Father's House." "He loveth most to whom most has been forgiven."

While sitting alone one day and pondering these things, and particularly the difficulty which people often find in correcting in themselves even the faults which they deplore, this pregnant sentence was spoken audibly to my inner hearing by a voice which I recognised as that of my Genius:— "Tendencies encouraged for ages cannot be cured in a single lifetime, but may require ages."

This further reflection also was suggested to me: that souls of exceptional strength are reincarnated in bodies of exceptionally strong passional natures, expressly in order to obtain the discipline which comes of the effort to subdue them. All of which reflections tended to exhibit the rashness of judging outward judgment in respect of others. In order to judge righteous judgment it is necessary to know the strength of their temptations, and of their efforts to resist them. And these can be known only to God. The attainment of perfection, and therein of salvation by conquest and not by flight,—this is the principle of reincarnation. It is the *condition* of Regeneration, which is *from out of* the body.

In due time we were able to recognise the whole plan of our work as so ordered as to make the work itself a demonstration of the doctrine of reincarnation. When once this doctrine had become a practical question for us, it assumed a prominent place both in our teachings and in our experiences. One instruction given us was no less striking in itself than in the circumstances of its communication. The messenger was one with whom we had never anticipated coming into relations, for, besides not courting intercourse with the souls of the departed, we had not paid to the writings of the person concerned the heed that would entitle us to count him among our cordial sympathisers; and still less as among our possible visitants. This was the famous Swedish Seer, Emmanuel Swedenborg. In the course of what we afterwards found to be a strikingly characteristic communication from him, he informed us that owing to the difficulty our angels had in approaching us just then, through the condition of the spiritual atmosphere, they had charged him with a message to us, in which "Mary's" Genius had spoken to him of her as "A soul of vast experience, who under his tuition had so painfully acquired the evangel of which she was the depositary"; adding that he, her Genius, "had been promised help to recover for her, in this incarnation, the memory of all that was in the past"; and—which was the point of the message—that it was to be put forward, not as we were then contemplating putting it forward, but "as fragmentary specimens of such recollection occurring to one now a woman, but formerly an initiate, who is beginning to recover this power."

It will be interesting to remark on this experience, that to this day the followers of Swedenborg set their faces against the doctrine of reincarnation, expressly on the ground that their master denied it in his lifetime. Whether Swedenborg really denied it is uncertain. There is grave cause to doubt whether his writings on the subject have been rightly understood or fairly represented. It has been maintained with much show of reason that Swedenborg denied only the reincarnation of the astral soul, not of the true soul; in which case he would be right. Having once obtained access to us, his visits were for a time frequent, the manner of them being various. For he came to us jointly and separately, in waking and in sleeping—the latter to "Mary" only—and audibly and visibly—the latter also to "Mary" only. He alluded to a recent incarnation of mine, of which I have since had full and independent proof. And he recognised our work as not only a confirmation and continuation of his own, but also as a correction. For, as he gave us to understand, he had been too much under the influence of the current orthodoxy to be able to transmit the revelation given to him in its proper purity, and unbiased by his own preconceptions. The doctrine in respect of which he was chiefly desirous of being set right was that of the Incarnation, the orthodox presentment of which he now saw to be wrong, by reason of its deification of Jesus. In referring to the perversion of the truth by the formulators of the Christian orthodoxy, he said to us, with much emphasis, "Do not be too kind to the Christians."

This allusion to an experience which belongs to the category of "spiritualism" rather than to that of our special work, may with advantage be followed by some account of our other experiences of the same order, partly for the sake of testifying to the genuineness of the experiences relied on by spiritualists, and partly in order to show the distinction between the two orders of experience, as discerned by persons whose familiarity with both qualified them to institute comparison between them. For, having once become sensitised in the inner and higher regions of the consciousness, we had become sensitised also in the intermediate regions, and were able therefore to hold palpable converse with the denizens of these also. And the converse thus held was of the most satisfactory character, on the ground both of the certainty of its reality and its intrinsic nature. Father, mother, wife, brothers, sundry dear friends, and others interested in our work, all came to me, and some of them to my colleague, and this several times, and in a manner impossible to be distrusted. For my mother more than once spoke to me aloud in her own unmistakeable voice, and in tones that anyone might have heard, as I sat alone in my study. My wife came repeatedly to both of us, jointly and separately, audibly, visibly, and tangibly; giving us timely warnings of dangers unsuspected by us but proving to be real. And one of my brothers cleared up a mystery which had hung over his death. No mere attenuated wraiths or soulless phantoms were they who thus visited us from "beyond the veil," they were strong, distinct, intelligent individualities, veritable souls, palpitating with vitality, and eager to render loving service. But they came spontaneously and unevoked, for we never sought to compel their presence. Our quest was purely and simply for truth, not for persons. But we considered that, when these also came, as they did come, to ourselves directly and without intervention of any third party, to refuse to receive them on the ground that they had put off their bodies, would be equivalent to repulsing our friends in the flesh on the ground that they had put off their overcoats.

The spirit in which alone such intercourse is permissible will be seen by the following citations from the instructions received by us. Terms from the Hebrew, Greek, and Oriental Scriptures were used indifferently by our illuminators. The word *Ruach* in the following—which is Hebrew for Spirit—is here used in a kabalistic sense to denote the astral soul or ghost, as distinguished from the divine soul, the *Psyche* or *Neshamah*, and from the *Nephesh* or mere phantom. The following is from an instruction given to "Mary" in sleep, in direct solution of certain perplexities.

"Thou knowest that in the end, when Nirvâna is attained, the soul shall gather up all that it hath left within the astral of holy memories and worthy experience, and to this end the Ruach rises in the astral sphere, by the gradual decay and loss of its more material affinities, until these have so disintegrated and perished that its substance is thereby lightened and purified. But continual commerce and intercourse with earth add, as it were, fresh fuel to its earthly affinities, keeping these alive, and hindering its recall to its spiritual ego. Thus, therefore, the spiritual ego itself is detained from perfect absorption into the divine, and union therewith. For the Ruach shall not all die, if there be in it anything worthy of recall. The astral sphere is its purging chamber. For Saturn, who is Time, is the trier of all things; he devoureth all the dross; only that escapeth which in its nature is ethereal and destined to reign. And this death of the Ruach is gradual and natural. It is a process of elimination and disintegration, often—as men measure time—extending over many decades, or even centuries. And those Ruachs which appertain to wicked and evil persons, having strong wills inclined earthwards,—these persist longest and manifest most frequently and vividly, because they *rise not*, but, being destined to perish utterly, are not withdrawn from immediate contact with the earth. They are all dross; there is in them no redeemable element. But the Ruach of the righteous complaineth if thou disturb his evolution. 'Why callest thou me? disturb me not. The memories of my earth-life are chains about my neck; the desire of the past detaineth me. Suffer me to rise towards my rest, and hinder me not with evocations. But let thy love go after me and encompass me; so shalt thou rise with me through sphere after sphere.'

"For the good man upon earth can love nothing less than the divine. Wherefore that which he loveth in his friend is the divine, that is, the true and radiant self. And if he love it as differentiated from God, it is only on account of its separate tincture. For in the perfect light there are innumerable tinctures. And according to its celestial affinity, one soul loveth this or that splendour more than the rest. And when the righteous friend of the good man dieth, the love of the living man goeth after the true soul of the dead; and the strength and divinity of this love helpeth the purgation of the astral soul, the psychic ghost. It is to this astral soul, which ever remaineth near the living friend, an indication of the way it must also go,—a light shining upon the upward path that leads from the astral to the celestial and everlasting. For love, being divine, is *towards* the divine. 'Love exalteth, love purifieth, love uplifteth.'"

And this also, which was similarly obtained, represents a further restoration of the original, pure, undistorted and unmutilated doctrine of Christianity concerning the communion of souls.

So weepest thou and lamentest, because the Soul thou lovest is taken from thy sight.

And life seemeth to thee a bitter thing: yea, thou cursest the destiny of all living creatures.

And thou deemest thy love of no avail, and thy tears as idle drops.

Behold, Love is a ransom, and the tears thereof are prayers.

And if thou have lived purely, thy fervent desire shall be counted grace to the soul of thy dead.

For the burning and continual prayer of the just availeth much.

Yea, thy love shall enfold the soul which thou lovest: it shall be unto him a wedding garment and a vesture of blessing.

The baptism of thy sorrow shall baptize thy dead, and he shall rise because of it.

Thy prayers shall lift him up, and thy tears shall encompass his steps: thy love shall be to him a light shining upon the upward way.

And the angels of God shall say unto him, "O happy Soul, that art so well-beloved; that art made so strong with all these tears and sighs.

"Praise the Father of Spirits therefor: for this great love shall save thee many incarnations.

"Thou art advanced thereby; thou art drawn aloft and carried upward by cords of grace."

For in such wise do souls profit one another and have communion, and receive and give blessing, the departed of the living, and the living of the departed.

And so much the more as the heart within them is clean, and the way of their intention is innocent in the sight of God....

Count not as lost thy suffering on behalf of other souls; for every cry is a prayer, and all prayer is power.

That thou willest to do is done; thine intention is united to the Will of Divine Love.

Nothing is lost of that which thou layest out for God and for thy brother.

And it is love alone who redeemeth, and love hath nothing of her own[46].

But precious as is the communion of souls when thus conditioned, it was not to them that we looked for light and guidance in our work. Nor, indeed, to any persons at all in the sense in which the term is ordinarily used. We looked steadfastly and directly to the Highest, confidently leaving to the Highest the appointment both of the Messenger and of the Message, but never failing to submit both manner and matter to the keenest scrutiny of faculties which we had striven to the utmost to attune to divine things. We were, moreover, emphatically warned from the outset against allowing any intrusion into our work of the influences accessible to the ordinary sensitive, the two planes being absolutely distinct. Herein lay the significance of the saying of "Mary's" Genius, that he had been "promised help to enable her to recover in this incarnation the memory of all that is in the past." The Genii themselves, although of the celestial, belong to its circumferential and lowest sphere. They touch the astral, but do not enter it. The help spoken of was to come from the innermost and highest spheres. And the charge was accordingly given us, "Do not, then, seek after 'controls.' Keep your temple for the Lord God of Hosts; and turn out of it the money-changers, the dove-sellers, and the dealers in curious arts, yea, with a scourge of cords if need be."

The manner in which we received the first full and particular account respecting the method of revelation, was as follows. I was pondering to myself with much intentness the nature and source of inspiration, and desiring a test whereby to distinguish between true and false inspiration. But I refrained for various reasons from consulting my colleague, at least until I should have exhausted my own resources. And she was still without any intimation of my need when she received the instruction concerning inspiration and prophesying of which the following is a portion. It was received in sleep, and the date was shortly before we were told that her knowledges were due to experiences undergone in previous lives[47]. When I had read it she said, referring to the first verse, "But I did not ask." In reply to which I told her that I had asked. It was addressed equally to both of us, as making together one system.

"I heard last night in my sleep a voice speaking to me, and saying—

"You ask the method and nature of Inspiration, and the means whereby God revealeth the Truth.

Know that there is no enlightenment from without: the secret of things is revealed from within.

From without cometh no Divine Revelation: but the Spirit within beareth witness.

Think not that I tell you that which you know not: for except you know it, it cannot be given to you.

To him that hath it is given, and he hath the more abundantly.

None is a prophet save he who knoweth: the instructor of the people is a man of many lives.

Inborn knowledge and the perception of things, these are the sources of revelation: the Soul of the man instructeth him, having already learned by experience.

Intuition is inborn experience; that which the soul knoweth of old and of former years.

And Illumination is the Light of Wisdom, whereby a man perceiveth heavenly secrets.

Which Light is the Spirit of God within the man, showing unto him the things of God.

Do not think that I tell you anything you know not; all cometh from within: the Spirit that informeth is the Spirit of God in the prophet.

Inspiration may indeed be mediumship, but it is conscious; and the knowledge of the prophet instructeth him.

Even though he speak in an ecstasy, he uttereth nothing that he knoweth not."

Then followed this apostrophe to the Prophet:—

"Thou who art a prophet hast had many lives: yea, thou hast taught many nations, and hast stood before kings.

And God hath instructed thee in the years that are past, and in the former times of the earth.

By prayer, by fasting, by meditation, by painful seeking, hast thou attained that thou knowest.

There is no knowledge but by labour: there is no intuition but by experience.

I have seen thee on the hills of the East: I have followed thy steps in the wilderness: I have seen thee adore at sunrise: I have marked thy night watches in the caves of the mountains.

Thou hast attained with patience, O prophet! God hath revealed the truth to thee from within."

Thus, for the first time known to history, was given a definition of the nature and method of inspiration and prophecy, at once luminous, reasonable, and inexpugnable, to the full and final solution of this stupendous problem; and comporting with and explaining, as it did, all our own experiences, we felt that we could bear unreserved testimony to its truth. But, vast as was the addition thus made to the New Gospel of Interpretation, it did not exhaust the treasures revealed and communicated on that wondrous night; for it was followed immediately by a prophecy of the meaning of the new dispensation on which the world is entering, and of which our work is the introduction. At once Biblical in diction and character, it reached in loftiness the highest level of Biblical prophecy and inspiration, demonstrating the same world celestial and divine as the source of both. For which reason, and the crushing blow administered by it to the superstitions which have made of Christianity a by-word and a reproach by their gross materialisations of mysteries purely spiritual, it is reproduced in full here. The heading is of our own devising:—

A Prophecy of the Kingdom of the Soul, mystically called the Day of the Woman.

"And now I show you a mystery and a new thing, which is part of the mystery of the fourth day of creation.

The word which shall come to save the world, shall be uttered by a woman.

A woman shall conceive, and shall bring forth the tidings of salvation.

For the reign of Adam is at its last hour; and God shall crown all things by the creation of Eve.

Hitherto the man hath been alone, and hath had dominion over the earth.

But when the woman shall be created, God shall give unto her the kingdom; and she shall be first in rule and highest in dignity.

Yea, the last shall be first, and the elder shall serve the younger.

So that women shall no more lament for their womanhood; but men shall rather say, "O that we had been born women!"

For the strong shall be put down from their seat, and the meek shall be exalted to their place.

The days of the Covenant of Manifestation are passing away: the Gospel of Interpretation cometh.

There shall nothing new be told; but that which is ancient shall be interpreted.

So that man the manifesto shall resign his office: and woman the interpreter shall give light to the world.

Hers is the fourth office: she revealeth that which the Lord hath manifested.

Hers is the light of the heavens, and the brightest of the planets of the holy seven.

She is the fourth dimension; the eyes which enlighten; the power which draweth inward to God.

And her kingdom cometh; the day of the exaltation of woman.

And her reign shall be greater than the reign of the man: for Adam shall be put down from his place; and she shall have dominion for ever.

And she who is alone shall bring forth more children to God, then she who hath an husband.

There shall no more be a reproach against women: but against men shall be the reproach.

For the woman is the crown of man, and the final manifestation of humanity.

She is the nearest to the throne of God, when she shall be revealed.

But the creation of woman is not yet complete: but it shall be complete in the time which is at hand.

All things are thine, O Mother of God: all things are thine, O Thou who risest from the sea; and Thou shalt have dominion over all the worlds[48].

CHAPTER IV.
THE ANTAGONISATION.

Even had we been disposed, which happily we were not, to exalt ourselves on the strength of the loftiness of our mission, the constant proofs afforded us of the paucity of our knowledge in comparison with what remained to be known, would have effectually restrained us. But as it was, we were from the first penetrated by the conviction that only in so far as we succeeded in subordinating the individual to the universal, the personal to the divine, could the work be successfully accomplished. The man must make himself nothing that the God may be all. This was the burden of the injunctions enforced on us throughout; the failures of others through self-exaltation being adduced in illustration. For, as we were plainly given to understand, "many are called but few are chosen"; the weak point in their system, the "Judas" by whom they are betrayed and fail, being generally vanity. They are as instruments which mistake themselves for the mind and hand which wield them.

Humility and Love, the violet and the red, these are the two extremes of the prism which comprise between them all the Seven Spirits of God. Blended, they make the royal purple; but the hue of that purple depends on the spiritual states of the individuals themselves whose tinctures they are. They were, we were told, the tinctures of our own souls as indicated by the colours of our respective *auras*. "Mary's" was the "blood-red ray of the innermost sphere," the sphere of the "first of the Gods," wherein "love and wisdom are one." "For the Hebrews Uriel, for the Greeks Phoibos, the Bright One of God." Mine was the violet of the outermost sphere, that of the "last of the Gods," the "Spirit of the Fear of the Lord," and therein of Reverence and Humility; for the Greeks Saturn, and for the Hebrews Satan, the "Angel unfallen of the outermost sphere." Only when man is built up of all the Gods, and bears upon him the seal of each God, having climbed the ladder of his regeneration from circumference to centre, from "Saturn" to the "Sun," is the "week" of his new and spiritual creation accomplished. Similarly the co-operation of all these divine potencies was indispensable to our work. And we were emphatically warned of the dangers both to it and to ourselves, that would come of the lack of the divine presence in respect of any of them. Hence the necessity of maintaining the necessary conditions in ourselves, and the caution addressed to us by "Hermes," in view of the liability of mortals to appropriate to themselves the importance appertaining to their mission when this transcends the ordinary. To this end, in the following Exhortation, he disclosed to us the heights yet to be ascended, saying—

He whose adversaries fight with weapons of steel, must himself be armed in like manner, if he would not be ignominiously slain or save himself by flight.

And not only so, but forasmuch as his adversaries may be many, while he is only one; it is even necessary that the steel he carries be of purer temper and of more subtle point and contrivance than theirs.

I, Hermes, would arm you with such, that bearing a blade with a double edge, ye may be able to withstand in the evil hour.

For it is written that the tree of life is guarded by a sword which turneth every way.

Therefore I would have you armed both with a perfect philosophy and with the power of the divine life.

And first the knowledge; that you and they who hear you may know the reason of the faith which is in you.

But knowledge cannot prevail alone, and ye are not yet perfected.

When the fulness of the time shall come, I will add unto you the power of the divine life.

It is the life of contemplation, of fasting, of obedience, and of resistance.

And afterwards the chrism, the power, and the glory. But these are not yet.

Meanwhile remain together and perfect your philosophy.

Boast not, and be not lifted up; for all things are God's, and ye are in God, and God in you.

But when the word shall come to you, be ready to obey.

There is but one way to power, and it is the way of obedience.

Call no man your master or king upon the earth, lest ye forsake the spirit for the form and become idolaters.

He who is indeed spiritual, and transformed into the divine image, desires a spiritual king.

Purify your bodies, and eat no dead thing that has looked with living eyes upon the light of Heaven.

For the eye is the symbol of brotherhood among you. Sight is the mystical sense.

Let no man take the life of his brother to feed withal his own.

But slay only such as are evil; in the name of the Lord.

They are miserably deceived who expect eternal life, and restrain not their hands from blood and death.

They are miserably deceived who look for wives from on high, and have not yet attained their manhood.

Despise not the gift of knowledge; and make not spiritual eunuchs of yourselves.

For Adam was first formed, then Eve.

Ye are twain, the man with the woman, and she with him, neither man nor woman, but one creature.

And the kingdom of God is within you[49].

The knowledge of the "Seven Spirits" whereby Deity operates in the universe, has been completely dropped out of sight by the Christian world. It is necessary, therefore, if only in vindication of the importance attached to them by our illuminators, to recite the instruction received by us concerning them, which is as follows. It is a chapter from the recovered Gnosis[50]:—

"In the bosom of the Eternal were all the Gods comprehended, as the seven spirits of the prism, contained in the Invisible Light.

By the Word of Elohim were the Seven Elohim manifest: even the Seven Spirits of God in the order of their precedence:

The Spirit of Wisdom, the Spirit of Understanding, the Spirit of Counsel, the Spirit of Power, the Spirit of Knowledge, the Spirit of Righteousness, and the Spirit of Divine Awfulness.

All these are coequal and coeternal.

Each has the nature of the whole in itself: and each is a perfect entity.

And the brightness of their manifestation shineth forth from the midst of each, as wheel within wheel, encircling the White Throne of the Invisible Trinity in Unity.

These are the Divine fires which burn before the presence of God: which proceed from the Spirit, and are one with the Spirit.

He is divided, yet not diminished: He is All, and He is One.

For the Spirit of God is a flame of fire which the Word of God divideth into many: yet the original flame is not decreased, nor the power thereof nor the brightness thereof lessened.

Thou mayest light many lamps from the flame of one; yet thou dost in nothing diminish that first flame.

Now the Spirit of God is expressed by the Word of God, which is Adonai.

For without the Word the Will could have had no utterance.

Thus the Divine Will divided the Spirit of God, and the seven fires went forth from the bosom of God and became seven spiritual entities.

They went forth into the Divine Substance, which is the substance of all that is."

As already stated, Hermes is the Greek name for the Second of the creative Elohim above enumerated. Hence his special relation to the New Gospel of Interpretation, the appeal of which is to the Understanding.

Being shown one day in vision the path we had to traverse for the accomplishment of our work, "Mary" exclaimed:—

"What a dreadfully difficult thing it is to steer one's way amidst such numbers of influences! I see a fine, bright-shining thread. It is our own path, and it is a pathway of light. But, oh! so narrow, so narrow, and all around are spirits trying to lure us from it. Here is Hermes, shining like a silver light. My Genius says that the way to get the utmost vitality on the spiritual plane is to abandon the plane of the body, and keep it quite low, by not indulging it. The time for bodily indulgence is passed with us. Abstinence, we have been told, and watchfulness and fasting are needful. And the time for the first of these has come. Nothing is gained without labour or won without suffering. Fasting and Watching and Abstinence, these are Beads and Rosary. It is a hard way and a long way, and it makes one wishful to turn back. We are not to be misled by the story, so much dwelt on to you by the Astrals, of Moses and Aaron[51]. They both were failures, who entered not into the land of Canaan. We must be patient and trust. We have to be cultivated on both planes, the intellectual and the spiritual, and not on the physical, for this draws from and saps the others."

So far as I was concerned, there was yet another rule that was made absolute: this was the rule of Poverty. Desiring at one time to mitigate the rigour of my enforced economies by working with a commercial intent, and to that end endeavouring to finish a tale some time before commenced, I found myself baffled by a complete withdrawal of power. I was well aware that no romance I could devise would compare with the romance I was living, and that any incidents I could invent would be tame before those of my actual life; but it was not this that withheld me. It was made clear to me that there was now only one direction and one plane in which I was accessible to ideas and in which therefore I could work, and this a direction and plane altogether incompatible with mundane ends. But I had not fully reconciled myself to the loss of my earning power, or resolved to refrain from further efforts in that behalf, when I received the following experience.

I had gone to bed, but not to sleep, for thinking over the matter, when I became aware of the presence of a group of spiritual influences, one of whom, speaking for them all, said to me, in tones audible only to the inner hearing, but distinct, measured and authoritative—

"We whom you know as the Gods—Zeus, Phoibos, Hermes, and the rest—are actual celestial personalities, who are appointed to represent to mortals the principles and potencies called the Seven Spirits of God. We have chosen you for our instrument, and have tried you and proved you and instructed you; and you belong to us to do our work and not your own, save in so far as you make it your own. Only in such measure as you do this will you have any success. For you can do nothing without us now: and it is useless for you to attempt to do anything without our help."

By this and manifold other experiences, we had practical demonstration of the existence of a celestial hierarchy consisting of souls perfected and divinised, divided into orders corresponding to the "Seven Spirits of God," and having for their function the illumination of those souls of men still on earth who are accessible by them; and to whom they manifest themselves in the forms recognised in the mysteries in which such persons have formerly been initiated.

We had also manifold proofs of their power to arrest utterance before persons unfit to be entrusted with the mysteries. The first instance occurred to myself, and was in this wise. I was reading some passages in illustration of our work to an old clerical friend who came to see me in Paris, when I inadvertently turned to a part of the book which we had been charged to keep secret. But before I had read a line, the air round me became so dense with invisible presences that I was unable to see, and my heart was clutched, as if by an invisible hand, and lifted up towards my throat with such force as almost to choke me; while, at the same instant, an overwhelming sense of my fault was impressed on my mind, causing me for some hours to feel as one utterly God-forsaken and cast off.

Not thinking that "Mary" was liable to err in the same way, or caring to tell her of my trespass, I kept silence respecting this experience. But a few weeks later it was repeated for her. She was speaking of our work to a spiritualist friend with whom we were spending the evening, and, in her eagerness, got upon topics which I recognised as forbidden. But before I had time to remind her, she suddenly stopped short and rose from her seat, gasping and dazed, and insisted on returning home forthwith, to our hostess's great amazement and disappointment. Divining what had occurred, I refrained from questioning her until we were outside and alone, when in reply to me she described exactly what had happened to me, using the words, "I did not want to be choked!" There were other occasions on which I was cut short under like circumstances, by having all that I meant to say suddenly and completely obliterated from my mind.

Being desirous to know more of the adverse influences against which we had been warned, and from which we suffered, "Mary" consulted her illuminator respecting their origin and nature, when the following colloquy ensued:—

"They are," he said, "the powers which affect and influence Sensitives. They do not control, for they have no force.... They are Reflects. They have no real entity in themselves. They resemble mists which arise from the damp earth of low-lying lands, and which the heat of the sun disperses. Again, they are like vapours in high altitudes, upon which, if a man's shadow falls, he beholds himself as a giant. For these spirits invariably flatter and magnify a man to himself. And this is a sign whereby you may know them. They tell one that he is a king; another, that he is a Christ; another, that he is the wisest of mortals, and the like. For, being born of the fluids of the body, they are unspiritual and live *of* the body."

"Do they, then," I asked, "come from within the man?"

"All things," he replied "come from within. A man's foes are they of his own household."

"And how," I asked, "may we discern the Astrals from the higher spirits?"

"I have told you of one sign;—they are flattering spirits. Now I will tell you of another. They always depreciate Woman. And they do this because their deadliest foe is the Intuition. And these, too, are signs. Is there anything strong? they will make it weak. Is there anything wise? they will make it foolish. Is there anything sublime? they will distort and travesty it. And this they do because they are exhalations of matter, and have no spiritual nature. Hence they pursue and persecute the Woman continually, sending after her a flood of vituperation like a torrent to sweep her away. But it shall be in vain. For God shall carry her to His throne, and she shall tread on the necks of them.

"Therefore the High Gods will give through a woman the Interpretation which alone can save the world. A woman shall open the gates of the Kingdom to mankind, because Intuition only can redeem. Between the Woman and the Astrals there is always enmity; for they seek to destroy her and her office, and to put themselves in her place. They are the delusive shapes who tempted the saints of old with exceeding beauty and wiles of love, and great show of affection and flattery. Oh! beware of them when they flatter, for they spread a net for thy soul."

"Am I, then, in danger from them?" I asked. "Am I, too, a Sensitive?" And he said,—

"No, you are a Poet. And in that is your strength and your salvation. Poets are the children of the Sun, and the Sun illumines them. No poet can be vain or self-exalted; for he knows that he speaks only the words of God. 'I sing,' he says, 'because I must.' Learn a truth which is known only to the sons of God. The Spirit within you is divine. It is God. When you prophesy and when you sing, it is the Spirit within you which gives you utterance. It is the 'New Wine of Dionysos.' By this Spirit your body is enlightened, as is a lamp by the flame within it. Now, the flame is not the oil, for the oil may be there without the light. Yet the flame cannot be there without the oil. Your body, then, is the lamp-case into which the oil is poured. And this— the oil—is your soul, a fine and combustible fluid. And the flame is the Divine Spirit, which is not born of the oil, but is conveyed to it by the hand of God. You may quench this Spirit utterly, and thenceforward you will have no immortality; but when the lamp-case breaks, the oil will be spilt on the earth, and a few fumes will for a time arise from it, and then it will expend itself and leave at last no trace. Some oils are finer and more spontaneous than others. The finest is that of the soul of the poet. And in such a medium the flame of God's Spirit burns more clearly and powerfully, and brightly, so that sometimes mortal eyes can hardly endure its brightness. Of such an one the soul is filled with holy raptures. He sees as no other man sees, and the atmosphere about him is enkindled. His soul becomes transmuted into flame; and when the lamp of his body is shattered, his flame mounts and soars, and is united to the Divine Fire. Can such an one, think you, be vain-glorious or self-exalted, and lifted up? Oh no; he is one with God, and knows that without God he is nothing. I tell no man that he is a reincarnation of Moses, of Elias, or of Christ. But I tell him that he may have the Spirit of these if, like them, he be humble and self-abased, and obedient to the Divine Word."

So far from our being sufficiently advanced to escape molestation from the sources thus indicated, there were times when we suffered much from their incursions, even to the hindrance, for the time being, of the work on which our whole hearts were set. Knowing that everything depended on our unanimity, they sought to make division between us, and what they lacked in force was more than made up for by subtlety[52]. Despite all our vigilance, they would insinuate themselves like barbed and poisoned arrows between the joints of our armour, there to rankle and envenom, so insidious were their suggestions. They did not flatter, but attacked us. So that it was a satisfaction to be assured that they attack those only who are worth attacking. The very nature of our work was such as to invite attack from them, being what they were.

Meanwhile, no experience was withheld that would serve to qualify us for what proved to be an essential part of our work, the "discerning of spirits" in the sense, not merely of perceiving them, but of distinguishing their nature and character. And always was the lesson given in a form which combined with its other features that of total unexpectedness. Especially important was it for us to be able to distinguish between the spirits *of* the astral, against which we were warned, and spirits *in* the astral, namely, souls which had not yet accomplished their emancipation, but were in course of doing so. But while as regarded the former we were left to fight the battle for ourselves, as regarded the latter there was a control exercised, and none were permitted to approach us save such as had a message of service which would minister to the solution of a present problem. Of this the following experience was an instance. It helped us to a yet fuller comprehension, both of the reasons which had dictated our association, and of the liabilities to be guarded against.

It was evening[53], and we were occupied in our respective tasks, and so entirely engrossed by them as to be disposed to resent any interruption, when "Mary" bent across the table, and speaking in a low tone, said to me, "There is a spirit in the room who wants to speak to us. Shall I let him?" I assented on the condition that he had something to tell us really worth hearing. She then became entranced, being magnetised by his presence; and after telling me that he spoke with a strong American accent and professed to be a "meta-physical doctor"—meaning, she supposed, a doctor in metaphysics—repeated the following after him; for I could neither see nor hear him:—

"You two have been put together for a work which you could not do separately. I have been shown a chart of your past histories, containing your characters and your past incarnations. She is of a highly active, wilful disposition, and represents the centrifugal force. You, Caro, are her opposite, and, being contemplative and concentrated, represent the centripetal force. Without her expansive energy you would become altogether indrawn and inactive in deed; and without your restraining influence she would go forth and become dissipated in expansiveness. So extraordinary is her outward tendency that nothing but such an organism as she now has could repress it and keep it within bounds. It is for the work she has to do that she has been placed in a body of weakness and suffering. She is the man—and you the woman—element in your joint system. I can see only her female incarnations, but she has been a man much oftener than a woman; while you have generally been a woman, and would be one now but for the work you have to do. Even as a woman she has always been much more man than woman, for her wilfulness and recklessness have led her into enterprises of incredible daring. Nothing restrained her when her will prompted her. She would wreck any work to follow that, and only by combination with your centripetal tendency can she do the present work. As a man she has been initiated, once, a long time ago, in Thebes, afterwards in India. The things she has done in her past lives! Well, *I* do not say they were wrong, for I do not hold the existence of moral evil. All things are allowed for good ends; but this is a difficult truth to express."

Here she spoke in her own person, having under his magnetism recovered her own vision and recollection, saying—

"O Caro! I can see your past. You have been—no, it is all wiped out. I cannot see it now. I am not allowed to see it. Why is this? I see my own past. I see India:—a magnificent glittering white marble temple, and elephants. How tame they are! They are all out, and feeding in a field or enclosure. And there are such a number of splendid red flowers, they are cactuses, and all prickly. The trees have all their foliage on the top, and such long stems. They are palms. The soil is of a white dust. And the sky is so clear and blue! But the heat is terrible. I see you again. Your colour is blue, inclining to indigo, owing to your want of expansiveness. But I cannot see your past, except that you are mostly a woman. And now I am by the Nile,—such a fine broad river!"

Here she returned to her normal consciousness, our visitor having taken his departure.

Subsequently, in March, 1881, under the influence of a higher illuminative power, she found herself as one of a group of initiates making solemn procession through the aisles of a vast Egyptian temple, and chanting in chorus the rituals which compose the marvellous "Hymn to the Planet-God, Iacchos"[54]. For, long as it is, she was able to reproduce it afterwards. It was thus, by her recovery of the memory of knowledges acquired in past existences, that the divine originals were recovered from which the Bible-writers largely derived at once their doctrine and their diction. This is not to say that these were mere borrowers and unilluminate. It is to say only that they recognised the divinity of a prior revelation, and regarded it as a common heritage. The truth is one.

Among the uses of the painful experience we were now undergoing[55] was this one. It put me on a track of thought of high value in enabling me to determine our respective positions in regard to our work. It was clearly the endeavour of the astral influences by which we were being assailed—the "haters of the mysteries" as our Genii called them[56]—to break down our work by destroying that perfect harmony between us which was the first condition of it. And all my endeavours failing to discover in myself the weak point which rendered us accessible to them, carefully as I sought there for it, I was forced to look for it in her, and was disposed to ascribe it to the survival from the far past of some defect of the affectional nature. For, as we were now learning, man has a dual heredity, that of his physical parentage and that of his spiritual selfhood. From the former of which he derives his outward characteristics; and from the latter his inward character. The experience just recited served to confirm the surmise, but it did something else besides. It suggested to me the following explanation of the situation as growing out of the exigencies of our work. That work had for its purpose the accomplishment of the prophesied downfall of the "world's sacrificial system." It meant war to the knife against all the orthodoxies at once, religious, social, scientific. It meant a death-"wrestle, not against flesh and blood, but against principalities, against powers, against the rulers of the darkness of this world, against spiritual wickedness in high places." It meant, in short, the destruction foretold by the prophets of "that great city," the world's materialistic system in Church, State, and Society, wherein the "Lord," the divinity in man, is ever systematically crucified, and its replacement by the "Holy City" or system which comes down from the heaven of a perfect ideal.

What, then, I asked myself, was the foremost moral need for the instruments of such a work? Surely it was Courage. But courage subsists under two modes. There is the courage which manifests itself in action and aggression, and there is the courage which manifests itself in endurance and resistance. The former is its masculine mode, the latter its feminine mode. The former connotes Will, the latter connotes Love. And these were the parts assigned respectively to us in our joint system. Will and Love united had made the world; disunited, they had ruined the world; reunited, they would redeem the world. As He and She, King and Queen, positive and negative, centrifugal and centripetal, they are the dual powers of all things, the constituent principles at once of God and of Man. The whole Universe is Humanity, for it is the manifestation of God, and they are the divine man and woman of all being; in their conjunction omnipotent for good, in their disjunction omnipotent for evil. And whereas it is the function of Will to inflict, it is the function of Love to bear. It is not, then, to the lack of these qualities that our troubles are due, but to the defect of them, the defect of our respective qualities.

The tension of feeling induced by the situation had for me reached a pitch at which I had cause for serious apprehension lest my organism prove unequal to the strain. For, resolute though I myself was to endure to the end, come what might, the effort involved had so greatly affected my organic system as nearly to double the number of the heart's pulsations, to the imminent risk of a rupture fatal to life or reason. Such was the emergency when, longing for light and aid, I received at night[57] the following experience, which I reproduce as recorded at the time:—

It seemed to me that I was sole spectator in some circus or hippodrome. And in the arena were some horses, seven in number, harnessed to a common centre, but all facing in different directions like the spokes of a wheel, and pulling frantically, so that the vehicle to which they were attached remained stationary between them, through their counterbalancing each other; while at the same time it seemed as if it must presently be dragged asunder into pieces. On looking at it more closely, the vehicle seemed to become a person who was attempting to drive the horses, but was unable to get them into a line; and, strange to say, the driver was one and identical both with the horses and the vehicle, so that it was a living person who was in danger of being torn asunder by creatures who were in reality himself. While wondering what this meant, some one addressed me and said that if I would do any good, I must help to control and direct the animals which were thus pulling their owner asunder. And that the only way to do this was by so disposing myself that I should be at one and the same time in the centre with the driver, to help him to curb and direct his steeds, and outside at their heads in order to compel their submission. And not only must I be indifferent to their ramping and chafing, I must even suffer myself to be struck and wounded and trampled upon to any extent without flinching; for only when I was so unconscious of self as to be indifferent as to what might happen to me, would they cease to have power against me. And the reason why I must be also in the centre was that only there could I effectually co-operate with the driver to enable him to do his part in directing what in reality were the forces, as yet unbroken in, of his own system, into the road it was necessary for us both to follow. We were destined to be fellow-travellers, and our journey was to be made together and with that team. It could not be made by one of us without the other, and the failure to effect a complete conjunction and co-operation would bring certain ruin to the hopes of both of us and of all who looked to us. The owner of the horses, I was assured, could not of himself control them, and I could only enable him to do so by an absolute surrender of myself.

Applying this vision to the situation, the moral was obvious so far as I was concerned, and I wondered whether "Mary" would receive anything equally suggestive for herself. In the morning, after remaining unusually late in her room, she silently handed me the following account of an experience which had similarly and simultaneously been received by her:—

"I was shown two stars near each other, both of them shining with a clear bright light, only that of one the light had a purple tinge, and of the other a blood colour; and a great Angel stood beside me and bade me look at them attentively. I did so, and saw that the stars were not round, but seemed to have a piece cut out of the globe of each of them. And I said to the Angel, 'The stars are not perfect; but instead of being round, they are uneven.' He told me to look again; and I did so, and saw that each globe was really perfect, but that in each a small portion remained dark so as to present the appearance of having a piece out; and I noticed that these dark portions of the two stars were turned towards each other. Upon this I looked to the Angel for the explanation.

And the Angel said to me, 'These stars derive their light not only from the sun but from each other. If there be darkness in one of them, the corresponding face of the other will likewise be darkened; and how shall either reflect perfectly the image of the sun if it be dark to its companion star? For how shall it respond to that which is above all, if it respond not to that which is nearest?'

And I said, 'Lord, if the darkness in one of these stars be caused by the darkness in its fellow, which of them was first darkened?'

Then he answered me and said, 'These stars are of different tinctures; one is of the sapphire, the other of the sardonyx. Of the first the atmosphere is cool and equable; of the other it is burning and irregular. The spirit of the first is as God towards man; the spirit of the second is as the soul towards God. The first loves; the second aspires. And the office of the spirit which loves is outwards; while the office of the spirit which aspires is upwards. The light of the first, which is blue, enfolds, and contains, and embraces, and sustains. The light of the second, which is red, is as a flame which scorches, and burns, and troubles, and seeks God only, and his duty is not to the outward, for it is not given to him to love. God, whom he seeks, *is* love; and therefore is he drawn upward to God only. But the spirit of his fellow descends. She indraws, and blesses, and confers; and hers is the office which redeems. Wherefore if she fail in her love, her failure is greater than his who hath no love; and to be perfect she must forgive until the seventy times seven, and be great in humility. For the violet, which is the colour of humility, is of the blue. And if she seek her own, or yield not in outward things, her nature is not perfected, and her light is darkened. Let

Love, therefore, think not of herself, for she hath no self, but all that she hath is towards others, and only in giving and forgiving is she rich. If, on the contrary, she make a self withinwards, her light is withdrawn and troubled, and she is not perfect, and if she demand of another that which he hath not, then she seeketh her own, and her light is darkened. And if she be darkened towards him, he also will darken towards her, in respect, that is, of enlightenment. And thus her failure of love will break the communion with the Divine, which is through him. He cannot darken outwardly first; for love is not of him. If he darken of himself, it must be within towards God. But that which he receives of God, he gives not forth himself. But he burns centrally and enlightens his fellow, and she gives it forth according to her office. And if she darken in any way outwardly, she cannot receive enlightenment, but darkens the burning star likewise, and so hinders their inter-communion.'

Having thus spoken, the Angel looked upon me and said, 'Ye are the two stars, and to one is given the office of the Prophet, and to the other the office of the Redeemer. But to be Prophet and Redeemer in one, this is the glory of the Christ.'"

Here again was an intimation that on one plane at least of our respective systems she was of masculine and I of feminine potency, with functions to correspond. That these functions were capable of being described in the terms employed was, we felt, no reason for arrogating high places to ourselves. Rather did we consider that everything is according to its degree; and that, as for persons, if the Gods were to wait until they found perfect instruments, or at least perfect persons for their instruments, they would never begin. And this also, that if the world were in a condition to produce such persons, it would have no need of redemption. Had not even Jesus Himself been "crucified through weakness"?

In view of the intensity of the distress undergone in this connection, I found myself recalling the remark of Plato, "Many begin the mysteries, but few complete them." My only wonder was that any should survive the ordeals, if they approached ours in severity. Meanwhile it was said to us by way of encouragement, "Be sure there is trouble in store. No man ever got to the Promised Land without first going through the wilderness."

The instruction to "Mary" had not only justified my surmise, it also met and corrected her in respect of the chief cause of our trouble. This was her disposition, at astral instigation, to withhold from me the products of her illuminations, and even to refrain from writing them down[58], on the specious pretext that they were meant for her own exclusive benefit, and were too sacred to be given to the world, or even to me; and she had failed to discern the source and motive of these suggestions. So effectually had what were really spirits of darkness disguised themselves as angels of light.

The importance attached to the occult significance of our "tinctures" received illustration in this wise. Permission had been given us to make an exception to the rule of secrecy imposed with regard to certain of the Scriptures received by us, in favour of a friend[59] who took so warm an interest in our work as to be eager to render it material aid in the future should occasion arise. It was her mission, she declared, to do so. But when the day appointed for the reading came, "Mary" was so ill that her going seemed to be impossible, and the question accordingly arose as to whether I might go alone and read them without her. We had no sooner begun to consider the point than she became entranced, and was shown a large open volume, the book of the Greater Mysteries to which our Scriptures belonged, surrounded by an Iris composed of all the colours of the rainbow. She was then shown the following lines, which I wrote down as she repeated them:—

"The one in Red guards his privileges, and claims to be present whatever is read.

For the air is filled with the haters of the Mysteries.

Therefore for your sake the chain must be complete;

And the Light must be refracted round you seven times.

He who is Red stands within the holy circle.

And the Violet guards the outermost.

For the Word is a Word of Mystery, and they who guard it are Seven.

Beware that nothing you hear be told unless the circle be perfect.

And this charge we lay upon you until the work be accomplished.

Fire and sword and war are against you; you walk in the midst of commotion.

And your life is in peril every hour until the words be completed."

Up to the latest moment of the interval before the appointment it seemed impossible for her to go. She then suddenly recovered as by miracle, and was able to attend the reading.

The liabilities of our position subsequently[60] received this further illustration. "Mary" was introduced in sleep, by her Genius, into an apartment in the spiritual world which purported to be the laboratory of William Lilly, the famous astrologer who had foretold the great plague and fire of London in 1666, in order to have her horoscope told by him, he still pursuing his favourite studies. On quitting him she caught sight of a pile of books, one of which contained the Gnosis we were in course of recovering. The following colloquy then ensued:—

"You also have these Scriptures!" she exclaimed.

"Yes," said he, "but I keep them for myself alone."

"And why so," she asked, "since, if you have them, they are for the learning of others likewise? Will you not rather communicate these saving truths to thirsty souls?"

"I will communicate them," said he, fixing his eyes on her intently, "when I can find Seven Men who for forty days have tasted no flesh, whose hands have shed no blood, and whose tongues have tasted of none."

"But if you find not Seven?"

"Then, mayhap, I shall find Five."

"And if not Five?"

"Then, maybe, I shall meet with Three."

"But even this may be hard to find, and if you should not meet with Three, what then will you do?"

"One Neophyte would not be able to protect himself."

In communicating to her the results of his calculations, he had said that owing to the propensities indulged in certain of her former lives, she had made for herself a destiny which ensured suffering and failure, except when living in a similar manner; doing which she would have a life of unbounded success. "But," he continued, "your horoscope has nothing for you but misfortune so long as you persist in a virtuous course of life, and, indeed, it is now too late to adopt another. I speak herein according to your Fortune, not in regard to your Inner life. With that I have no concern. I tell you what is forecast for you on the material and actual planisphere of your Nativity.... I see nothing but misfortune before you. Yea, if you persist in virtue, it is not unlikely that you may be stript of all your worldly goods, and of all you possess, and this evil fortune will follow your nearest associates."

To her enquiry, "Can I never overcome this evil prognostic?" he replied that she could do so only by outliving the time appointed for her natural life in the career indicated, and added this advice, "Steel yourself; learn to suffer; become a Stoic; care not. If Misfortune be yours, make it your Fortune. Let Poverty become to you Riches. Let Loss be Gain. Let Sickness be Health. Let Pain be Pleasure. Let Evil Report be Good Report. Yea, let

Death be Life. Fortune is in the Imagination. If you believe you have all things, they are truly yours." He concluded with an explanation reconciling destiny with free will, and vindicating the divine justice, in a manner which removed all our difficulties on those points, and, as we later came to learn, was entirely in accordance with the Hindu doctrine of "Karma," of which at this time we had never heard[61].

There was no exaggeration in the terms of the warning of danger. We were constantly made aware of the presence of the malignant entities above described focusing their influences on us to prevent the accomplishment of our work, and requiring the utmost vigilance on our part, as well also as on the part of our illuminators, to thwart their purpose. And we had good reason to believe that our difficulties and dangers were enhanced through "Mary's" attendances at the schools and hospitals, owing to the evil nature of the influences there dominant under a regimen grossly materialistic, and her liability to be fastened upon and accompanied home by them. The outer walls of her spiritual system—it was explained to us—were not yet completed, owing to the vastness of the circuit of her selfhood; and hence her accessibility to the incursion of noxious influences from without. The treatment of the patients by men trained in the physiological laboratory, and bent upon turning the hospital ward also into a laboratory with the patients themselves for the victims of cruel and wanton experimentation, would send her home boiling with indignation and wrath, to the destruction of the serenity and self-control requisite for our spiritual work.

It was clear to us that no experience was to be wanting to exhibit the contrast between the world's actual and the world's possible. The overthrow of "the world's sacrificial system" meant salvation for man and beast. The condition of all really redemptive work is a "descent into hell." The following instruction to us is a typical one:—

"Teach the doctrine of the Universal Soul and the Immortality of all creatures. Knowledge of this is what the world most needs, and this is the keynote of your joint mission. On this you must build; it is the key-stone of the arch. The perfect life is not attainable for man alone. The whole world must be redeemed under the new gospel you are to teach."

The following "Counsel of Perfection" which was received[62] by "Mary," is an exquisite expression of the same theme:—

I dreamed that I was in a large room, and there were in it seven persons, all men, sitting at one long table; and each of them had before him a scroll, some having books also; and all were greyheaded and bent with age save one, and this was a youth of about twenty, without hair on his face. One of the aged men, who had his finger on a place in a book open before him, said:

"This spirit, who is of our order, writes in this book,—'Be ye perfect, therefore, as your Father in heaven is perfect.' How shall we understand this word 'perfection'?" And another of the old men, looking up, answered, "It must mean Wisdom, for wisdom is the sum of perfection." And another old man said, "That cannot be; for no creature can be wise as God is wise. Where is he among us who could attain to such a state? That which is part only, cannot comprehend the whole. To bid a creature to be wise as God is wise would be mockery."

Then a fourth old man said:—"It must be Truth that is intended; for truth only is perfection." But he who sat next the last speaker answered, "Truth also is partial; for where is he among us who shall be able to see as God sees?"

And the sixth said, "It must surely be Justice; for this is the whole of righteousness." And the old man who had spoken first, answered him:— "Not so; for justice comprehends vengeance, and it is written that vengeance is the Lord's alone."

Then the young man stood up with an open book in his hand and said:—"I have here another record of one who likewise heard these words. Let us see whether his rendering of them can help us to the knowledge we seek." And he found a place in the book and read aloud:—

"Be ye merciful, even as your Father is merciful."

And all of them closed their books and fixed their eyes upon me.

That it was possible at all for her to study medicine in a school in which vivisection was an all prevailing practice, was only because she set her face resolutely against it, by refusing to attend any place or occasion where or on which it took place, and relying for her own education chiefly on private tuition. It was an essential part of her plan to prove that such experimentation was not necessary for a degree. And this she effectually demonstrated by accomplishing her student-course with rare expedition and distinction, despite her many and severe illnesses and her frequent change of professors. For one after another resigned the office on account of her refusal to allow them to experiment on live animals at her lessons. Not until she had secured her diploma did she enter a physiological laboratory. And then only in order to qualify herself by personal experience to denounce the practice. For herself it was not necessary, she declared, to see a murder or a robbery committed to know that it is a crime.

The following incident shows how adverse the conditions of modern life were to our spiritual work:—

Being in London one Christmas evening[63], and speaking to me under illumination, "Mary" suddenly broke off and said—

"Do not ask me such deep questions just now, for I cannot see clearly, and it hurts me to look. The atmosphere is thick with the blood shed for the season's festivities. The Astral Belt is everywhere dense with blood. My Genius says that if we were in some country where the conditions of life are purer, we could live in constant communication with the spiritual world. For the earth here whirls round as in a cloud of blood like red fire. He says distinctly and emphatically that the salvation of the world is impossible while people nourish themselves on blood. The whole globe is like one vast charnel-house. The magnetism is intercepted. The blood strengthens the bonds between the Astrals and the Earth.... This time, which ought to be the best for spiritual communion, is the worst, on account of the horrid mode of living. Pray wake me up: I cannot bear looking; for I see the blood and hear the cries of the poor slaughtered creatures." Here her distress was so extreme that she wept bitterly, and some days passed before she fully recovered her composure.

Our first acquaintance with any literature kindred to our special work took place toward the close of our sojourn in Paris[64]. It was due to the arrival of the friend in whose favour the exception had been made in respect of the reading of our Mysteries, and who was the possessor of an excellent library, which she placed at our disposal, of precisely the books it had now become necessary for us to read. This was Marie, Countess of Caithness and Duchesse de Pomár, who had for many years been a spiritualist of zeal so ardent that—as I now came to learn—she had been wont to make my conversion to that faith a matter of special prayer, long before I had been able to contemplate such an event as within the range of probability. Of wide culture, open mind, and large sympathies, she had an enthusiastic and intelligent appreciation of our work, and her arrival on the scene proved so timely as to point to superior direction. We were now able to begin to make acquaintance with many of the seers, mystics, and occultists of past ages, from the Neoplatonists, Hermetists, Rosicrucians, and other orders of initiates, to Bœhme, Swedenborg and "Eliphas Levi," and to see what the various spiritualistic schools of the present day had to say for themselves.

The following recognition of Hermes by one of the greatest of the Neoplatonists, Proclus, who lived in the fifth century of our era, was especially gratifying to us as proving the continuity of our experiences with those of past ages. Proclus, it must be remembered, was so eminent for his wisdom and powers as to be regarded by his contemporaries with a veneration approaching to adoration. Says Proclus, "Hermes, as the messenger of God, reveals to us His paternal Will, and—developing in us the Intuition—imparts to us knowledge. The knowledge which descends into the soul from above, excels any that can be attained by the mere exercise of the intellect. Intuition is the operation of the soul. The knowledge received through it from above, descending into the soul, fills it with the perception of the interior causes of things. The Gods announce it by their presence, and by illumination, and enable us to discern the universal order." Here was exactly the doctrine received by us, and the manner of it, only that the Intuition was further disclosed to us as due to interior recollection, as declared by Plato, as well as to perception.

The results of the investigations thus begun, and afterwards continued in the library of the British Museum, proved satisfactory and gratifying beyond all that we could have anticipated. For while it was made clear to us that there had never been a time when there were not some in the world who had the witness to the truth in themselves, and this one and the same truth, it was also made clear that whereas others had received it in limitation, and beheld it as "through a glass darkly," we were receiving it in plenitude and "face to face," to the realisation of the high anticipations of the sages, saints, seers, prophets, redeemers, and Christs of all time; and this, too, at the period, in the manner, and under the conditions declared by them as to mark and make the "time of the end."

For in the illuminations vouchsafed to us the key had been restored which unlocked the meaning of the symbols in which the doctrines of all the churches, pre-Christian as well as Christian, had been at once concealed and revealed, to the elucidation of all the problems which have so sorely perplexed the world, and the verification, by actual experience, of the truth contained in them. No longer now was there for us any doubt as to the meaning of allegories such as the Fall, the Deluge, the Exodus, and others were now shown us to be; or of prophecies such as those of the crushing of the serpent's head by the Woman and her seed; the return of Astræa with her progeny of divine sons; the fall from heaven of Lucifer and Satan; the Return of the Gods; the reign of Michael, "that great prince who standeth for the children of God's people"; the breaking of the seals, and opening of the books; the recognition of the abomination of desolation standing in the holy place; the budding of the fig-tree, and the end of that "adulterous generation"; the revelation of "that wicked one, the mystery of iniquity and son of perdition, whom the Lord, at His coming in the clouds of heaven with power and great glory, shall consume with the spirit of His mouth, and destroy with the brightness of His coming"; the two Witnesses, their resurrection from the dead, and their ascent into heaven; the drying up of the great river Euphrates, and the coming of the kings of the East by the way thus prepared; the binding of Satan, and the acceptable year of the Lord to follow; the exaltation to heaven, and clothing with the sun, of the mystic "Woman" of the Apocalypse; the advent of the angel flying in mid-heaven, having an eternal gospel to proclaim unto every nation, and tribe, and tongue, and people; the coming of many from the East, and the West, and the North, and the South, to sit down with Abraham, Isaac, and Jacob, in the kingdom of heaven; and the battle of Armageddon, and the end of the world. To all these, and other sacred enigmas of like nature, the key had been given us. And they one and all proved to be prophecies of one and the same event, the restoration of the faculty of inward understanding, and of the divine knowledges which only through it are possible. And whereas this was the faculty, the corruption and loss of which had made the Fall, which was that of the original Church, so was it the faculty, the purification and restoration of which was to reverse the Fall, accomplishing the Redemption. For by it man will regain his mental balance, in virtue of which he was "made upright," and become again sound, whole, and sane, and be by *condition* that which he has been divinely declared from the first to be by *constitution*,—an instrument of understanding, competent for the comprehension of all truth. For only thus is he really man, and made in the divine image; seeing that he is not really man, but infant only, until he attains his spiritual majority and is able to understand. And that which thus makes him man on the plane mental and spiritual, is that which makes him man on the plane physical. It is his recognition and appropriation of the "Woman" of that plane, the mystic "Woman" of Holy Writ, the mind's feminine mode, the Intuition. It is of her first identification by us, as the key to the whole mystery of the Bible, that the manner will now be recounted.

CHAPTER V.
THE RECAPITULATION.

The first compendious statement of the doctrine which it was intended to restore, was given to us at Paris in the summer of 1878, in the form of an exposition of the principles of Biblical interpretation, under the following circumstances.

We had been following our respective tasks[65] for several months without any open or special illumination, and I had written enough to make a considerable volume in exposition of the principles which appeared to me to be those on which, in order to be a book of the soul, the Bible ought to be constructed, and by which, therefore, it must be interpreted. It was not intended for publication, but as an exercise for myself, being purely tentative; though I was conscious of being aided by the occasional suggestion of ideas which served as points of light and guidance. Meanwhile, I was entirely without help from books; for, besides being desirous of evolving the whole from my own consciousness, as in the case of the demonstration of any mathematical problem, I was not aware of any books which would help me; the little I knew of Swedenborg at this time—who was the only writer known to me as a worker in a similar direction—having failed to make much impression on me. I could accept his general principles, but not his particular applications of them. I felt also that the sources of the knowledges vouchsafed to us, far transcended those to which Swedenborg had access. And I accounted for the length of the interval which had elapsed without any larger measure of light being vouchsafed, by supposing that it was intended for me to exhaust my own resources first.

The time had come when these were exhausted, and I was reduced to the conviction that if the work was to be carried any further, assistance must be rendered, whether for confirmation, for correction, or for extension. And on retiring to rest one night[66], painfully oppressed by the sense of my own lack, and the prolonged absence of the needed light, I stood at the open window, and in presence of a sky resplendent with stars mentally addressed to those whom we were wont to speak of as the Gods, and of whose presence I seemed to be dimly conscious, a strong expression of my need, declaring my utter inability to advance another step unassisted. Having done which I went to bed, but in a mood the reverse of sanguine; so many were the months for which they had been silent.

In the course of the following day, "Mary"—who knew nothing either of my need or of my adjuration of the preceding night, and could not of herself have helped me—found herself under an access of exaltation of faculty which she described as resembling what might be produced by a draught of spiritual champagne. For she felt herself at her very best, having all her knowledge at her finger-ends. The expression recurred to my mind some time afterwards on our receiving an explanation of the "New Wine of Dionysos" in the ancient mysteries. In this state she went down to the schools, where an examination in her subjects was being held, in order to see how the candidates comported themselves, and to compare them with herself; for it was an oral examination. From this she returned home in high delight, declaring that she could have answered every question asked, and far better than any of the students had done. I hoped that her state might be an indication of the renewal of her illuminations. But the events of the evening put all thoughts in this direction entirely out of my mind. For, as if poisoned by the atmosphere of the schools, she was seized with an attack of sickness so intense and prolonged as seriously to endanger her life through the exhaustion induced. And it was a late hour—past midnight—before she could be left alone.

Nevertheless she was up betimes in the morning, and on our meeting handed me a paper which she had written in pencil on waking, saying it was something she had read in her sleep, and asking if it was anything that I wanted, as she had written it down so rapidly that she scarcely observed what it was about, and she had not had time to read it over and think about it. Having read it, I found that it met my every difficulty, and shed on the Bible a light which rendered it luminous from beginning to end, disclosing it as pervaded by a system of thought which, when once seen, was as obvious as it had previously been unsuspected.

And while it confirmed me in respect of principles and method, it corrected both of us in respect of sundry particulars. It even referred directly to one of my tentative hypotheses, at once negativing it and giving another altogether satisfactory. This was my supposition of Adam and Eve as possibly denoting spirit and matter. The following is the writing:—

"If, therefore, they be Mystic Books, they ought also to have a mystic consideration. But the fault of most writers lieth in this,—that they distinguish not between the books of Moses the prophet, and those books which are of an historical nature. And this is the more surprising because not a few of such critics have rightly discerned the esoteric character, if not indeed the true interpretation, of the story of Eden; yet have they not applied to the remainder of the allegory the same method which they found to fit the beginning; but so soon as they are over the earlier stanzas of the poem, they would have the rest of it to be of another nature.

"It is, then, pretty well established and accepted of most authors, that the legend of Adam and Eve, and of the miraculous tree and the fruit which was the occasion of death, is, like the story of Eros and Psyche, and so many others of all religions, a parable with a hidden, that is, with a mystic meaning. But so also is the legend which follows concerning the sons of these mystical parents, the story of Cain and Abel his brother, the story of the Flood, of the Ark, of the saving of the clean and unclean beasts, of the rainbow, of the twelve sons of Jacob, and, not stopping there, of the whole relation concerning the flight out of Egypt. For it is not to be supposed that the two sacrifices offered to God by the sons of Adam, were real sacrifices, any more than it is to be supposed that the apple which caused the doom of mankind, was a real apple. It ought to be known, indeed, for the right understanding of the mystical books, that in their esoteric sense they deal, not with material things, but with spiritual realities; and that as Adam is not a man, nor Eve a woman, nor the tree a plant in its true signification, so also are not the beasts named in the same books real beasts, but that the mystic intention of them is implied. When, therefore, it is written that Abel took of the firstlings of his flock to offer unto the Lord, it is signified that he offered that which a lamb implies, and which is the holiest and highest of spiritual gifts. Nor is Abel himself a real person, but the type and spiritual presentation of the race of the prophets; of whom, also, Moses was a member, together with the Patriarchs. Were the prophets, then, shedders of blood? God forbid; they dwelt not with things material, but with spiritual significations. Their lambs without spot, their white doves, their goats, their rams, and other sacred creatures, are so many signs and symbols of the various graces and gifts which a mystic people should offer to Heaven. Without such sacrifices is no remission of sin. But when the mystic sense was lost, then carnage followed, the prophets ceased out of the land, and the priests bore rule over the people. Then, when again the voice of the prophets arose, they were constrained to speak plainly, and declared in a tongue foreign to their method, that the sacrifices of God are not the flesh of bulls or the blood of goats, but holy vows and sacred thanksgivings, their mystical counterparts. As God is a spirit, so also are His sacrifices spiritual. What folly, what ignorance, to offer material flesh and drink to pure power and essential being! Surely in vain have the prophets spoken, and in vain have the Christs been manifested!

"Why will you have Adam to be spirit, and Eve matter, since the mystic books deal only with spiritual entities? The tempter himself even is not matter, but that which gives matter the precedence. Adam is, rather, intellectual force: he is of earth. Eve is the moral conscience: she is the mother of the living. Intellect, then, is the male, and Intuition the female principle. And the sons of Intuition, herself fallen, shall at last recover Truth, and redeem all things. By her fault, indeed, is the moral conscience of humanity made subject to the intellectual force, and thereby all manner of evil and confusion abounds, since her desire is unto him, and he rules over her until now. But the end foretold by the seer is not far off. Then shall the Woman be exalted, clothed with the Sun, and carried to the throne of God. And her sons shall make war with the dragon, and have victory over him. Intuition, therefore, pure and a virgin, shall be the mother and redemptress of her fallen sons, whom she bore under bondage to her husband the intellectual force."

This marvellously luminous exposition, she then told me, had been read by her in a book she had found in a library which she had visited in sleep, the owner of which was a courtly old gentleman in the costume of the last century. The leaves of the book were of silver and reflected her back to herself as she read. I took this as symbolising the Intuition. The event proved that her host was no other than Swedenborg, and that—as her Genius informed us—she had been enabled, "under the magnetism of Swedenborg's presence, to recover a memory of no small value," thus confirming my surmise about its intuitional character. The event proved also that it was Swedenborg's doctrine, but without his limitations. We ardently desired a continuation of it, and on the next night but one, she received the following addition to it:—

"Moses, therefore, knowing the mysteries of the religion of the Egyptians, and having learned of their occultists the value and signification of all sacred birds and beasts, delivered like mysteries to his own people. But certain of the sacred animals of Egypt he retained not in honour, for motives which were equally of mystic origin. And he taught his initiated the spirit of the heavenly hieroglyphs, and bade them, when they made festival before God, to carry with them in procession, with music and with dancing, such of the sacred animals as were, by their interior significance, related to the occasion. Now, of these beasts, he chiefly selected males of the first year, without spot or blemish, to signify that it is beyond all things needful that man should dedicate to the Lord his intellect and his reason, and this from the beginning, and without the least reserve. And that he was very wise in teaching this, is evident from the history of the world in all ages, and particularly in these last days. For what is it that has led men to renounce the realities of the spirit, and to propagate false theories and corrupt sciences, denying all things save the appearance which can be apprehended by the outer senses, and making themselves one with the dust of the ground? It is their intellect which, being unsanctified, has led them astray; it is the force of the mind in them, which, being corrupt, is the cause of their own ruin, and of that of their disciples. As, then, the intellect is apt to be the great traitor against heaven, so also is it the force by which men, following their pure intuition, may also grasp and apprehend the truth. For which reason it is written that the Christs are subject to their mothers. Not that by any means the intellect is to be dishonoured; for it is the heir of all things, if only it be truly begotten and be no bastard.

"And besides all these symbols, Moses taught the people to have beyond all things an abhorrence of idolatry. What, then, is idolatry, and what are false gods?

"To make an idol is to materialise spiritual mysteries. The priests, then, were idolaters, who coming after Moses, and committing to writing those things which he by word of mouth had delivered unto Israel, replaced the true things signified, by their material symbols, and shed innocent blood on the pure altars of the Lord.

"They also are idolaters who understand the things of sense where the things of the spirit are alone implied, and who conceal the true features of the Gods with material and spurious presentations. Idolatry is materialism, the common and original sin of men, which replaces spirit by appearance, substance by illusion, and leads both the moral and intellectual being into error, so that they substitute the nether for the upper, and the depth for the height. It is that false fruit which attracts the outer senses, the bait of the serpent in the beginning of the world. Until the mystic man and woman had eaten of this fruit, they knew only the things of the spirit, and found them suffice. But after their fall, they began to apprehend matter also, and gave it the preference, making themselves idolaters. And their sin, and the taint begotten of that false fruit, have corrupted the blood of the whole race of men, from which corruption the sons of God would have redeemed them."

She had received this, also in sleep, as one of a class of neophytes seated in an ancient amphitheatre of white stone, and listening to a lecture delivered by a man in priestly garb, of which they took notes the while. She complained that her notes had disappeared on waking, thus preventing her from rendering what she had heard as perfectly as she could have wished; for she had trusted to her notes for it.

The more we pondered these communications, the higher was our appreciation of them. We felt that the "veil of Moses" was at length "taken away" as promised, and we had been enabled to tap a reservoir of boundless wisdom and knowledge. For we found in them the longed-for solution of the purpose and nature of the Bible and Christianity, and the key to man's spiritual history. The method of the Bible-writers, the meaning of idolatry, the secret of the Cain and Abel feud between priest and prophet, as the ministers respectively of the sense-nature and of the intuition, and the process whereby the religion of Jesus had become distorted into the orthodoxy which has usurped His name;—all these things were now clear to us as the demonstration of a proposition in geometry, the witness of which was in our own minds. And we, too, rejoiced to think, were of the school of the prophets, in that with all the force of our minds we had "exalted the Woman," Intuition, and refused to make the word of God of none effect by priestly traditions.

Not the least marvellous element in the case was the faculty whereby the seeress had been able to reproduce, after waking, with such evident faithfulness the things seen and heard at so great length in sleep. In reply to my questionings she said that the words seemed to show themselves to her again as she wrote[67].

Discoursing with her Genius on this subject of memory, she received the following, which is valuable also for its recognition of the mystical import of the Bible narratives, and confirmation of St Paul when he says in reference to certain narratives in Genesis, "These things are an allegory."

"Concerning memory; why should there any more be a difficulty in respect of it? Reflect on this saying,—'Man sees as he knows.' To thee the deeps are more visible than the surfaces of things; but to men generally the surfaces only are visible. The material can perceive only the material, the astral the astral, and the spiritual the spiritual. It all resolves itself, therefore, into a question of condition and of quality. Thy hold on matter is but slight, and thine organic memory is feeble and treacherous. It is hard for thee to perceive the surfaces of things and to remember their aspect. But thy spiritual perception is the stronger for this weakness, and the profound is that which thou seest the most readily. It is hard for thee to understand and to retain the memory of material facts; but their meaning thou knowest instantly and by intuition, which is the memory of the soul. For the soul takes no pains to remember; she knows divinely. Is it not said that the immaculate woman brings forth without a pang? The sorrow and travail of conception belong to her whose desire is unto 'Adam'"[68].

The following sentences sum up the conclusions to which, by degrees, we were led. The first two paragraphs are from an exposition concerning the dogma of the Immaculate Conception which we considered as one of the most sublime and momentous of all her illuminations[69].

"All that is true is spiritual.... No dogma is real that is not spiritual. If it be true, and yet seem to you to have a material signification, know that you have not solved it. It is a mystery; seek its interpretation. That which is true is for Spirit alone.

"For matter shall cease and all that is of it, but the Word of the Lord shall remain for ever. And how shall it remain except it be purely spiritual; since, when matter ceases, it would then be no longer comprehensible?"

"For, though matter is eternally the mode whereby spirit manifests itself, matter is not itself eternal."

"The church has all the truth, but the priests have materialised it, making religion idolatry, and themselves and their people idolaters."

"In their real and divinely intended sense, its doctrines are eternal verities, founded in the nature of Being. As ecclesiastically propounded, they are blasphemous absurdities."

"All the mistakes made about the Bible arise out of the mystic books being referred to times, places, and persons material, instead of being regarded as containing only eternal verities about things spiritual."

"The Bible was written by intuitionalists, for intuitionalists, and from the intuitionalist standpoint. It has been interpreted by externalists, for externalists, and from the externalist standpoint. The most occult and mystical of books, it has been expounded by persons without occult knowledge or mystical insight"[70].

Thus gradually but surely we learnt that Ecclesiastical education has rigidly excluded from its curriculum all those branches of study which could throw light on the real nature of existence, and consists in learning what other men have said who, themselves, did not know, but were mere hearsay scholars lacking the witness in themselves.

We marvelled much as to how the priesthoods will comport themselves when compelled to recognise the fact that a New Gospel of Interpretation has actually been vouchsafed from the world celestial in correction of their perversion and mutilation of the former Gospel of Manifestation, and suppression of the true doctrine of salvation. Will Cain and Caiaphas still have the dominion, and ecclesiasticism be as ready to crucify the Christ on His second coming as it was on His first? And if not, how will it find courage to face the world with the humiliating confession that all through the long ages of its history, while arrogantly claiming to be the faithful and infallible minister of the Gospel of Christ, it has persistently withheld that gospel, and, losing the key to its meaning, has substituted for the wholesome "bread" of divine truth, the "stones" of innutritious because unintelligible dogmas; and for the "fish" of the living waters, the "serpents" of the letter which kills? and that when men have rightly suspected that

Christianity has failed, not because it is false, but because it has been falsified, and have sought to their own inner light for the truth of which ecclesiasticism had defrauded them, it dealt out to them pitiless anathema and persecution, making the earth a scene of torture and slaughter in assertion of the right of the priesthoods to teach wrong?

That the work committed to us implied nothing less than the fulfilment of the prophecies of which the promise of the Second Coming of Christ was the culmination, while intimated to us from the outset, was gradually unfolded into full assurance, and we were enabled to see that the very terms in which it was couched implied a spiritual advent, and one which should disclose the perfect system at once of science, philosophy, morality, and religion, of which Christ is both the foundation and the consummation. For the "clouds of heaven" in which it was to take place, were no other than the heaven of the kingdom within man of his restored spiritual consciousness. "That wicked one," "the son of perdition," and "mystery of iniquity" then to be revealed and destroyed, was no other than the inspiring evil spirit of an ecclesiasticism which had received indeed its doctrines from above, but their interpretation and application from below. And the "Spirit of His mouth," and the "Brightness of His Coming" were no other than a new Word of God, in the form of a New Gospel of Interpretation, so potent in its logic and so luminous in its exposition as to indicate the Logos Himself as its source, and the "Woman" Intuition, "clothed with the Sun" of full illumination, as its revealer.

We saw, too, that with this "Woman" thus rehabilitated, God's "Two Witnesses,"—who have so long lain dead in the streets of "that great city" wherein the Lord, the divinity in man, is ever systematically crucified; the city of the world's system as fashioned and controlled by an ecclesiasticism shrouded in the threefold veil of Blood, Idolatry, and the Curse of Eve,— will rise and stand on their feet, and ascend to the heaven of their proper supremacy, *vice* Lucifer deposed and fallen. And in them Lucifer himself will regain his lost estate, vindicating his title to be called the Light-bearer, the bright and morning star, the herald and bringer-in of the perfect day of the Lord God. For, as the Intellect, he is the heir of all things, if only he be begotten of the Spirit, and be no bastard engendered of the Sense-Nature.

For—as we had come to learn—God's Two Witnesses in man are ever the Intellect and the Intuition, when duly unfolded and united in a pure spirit. Under such conditions the Shiloh comes, and mounted on them man rides triumphant as king into the holy city of his own regenerate nature. But divorced from her, the Intuition, and—leagued with the Sense-Nature— knowing matter only and the body, the Intellect becomes "prince of devils" in man, the maker of men into fiends, and of the earth into a hell.

Wherefore his fall from the heaven of his power, on the advent of that whole Humanity, of whom it is said, "the Man is not without the Woman, nor the Woman without the Man, in the Lord," the humanity of intellect and intuition combined, has ever been exultingly hailed in anticipation by all true seers and prophets.

The chief points of the doctrine, the prospect of the restoration of which has thus been the sustaining hope of the percipient faithful in all ages, may be summarised as follows:—

The doctrine which, first and foremost, it is the purpose of the Bible to affirm, and of the Christ to demonstrate, and in which reason entirely concurs, is no other than that of the divine potentialities of man, belonging to him in virtue of the nature of his constituent principles, the force and the substance of existence. These are the duality of the "heavens" which God is said to "create," meaning to put forth from Himself, "in the beginning," and of the mutual interaction of which all things are the product, varying according to the plane of operation, alike for creation and redemption, generation and regeneration. And that which Jesus really affirmed in the memorable but little understood words, "Ye *must* be born again, or from above, of Water and the Spirit," was both the possibility and the necessity to all men of realising the potential divinity belonging to them in virtue of the divinity of their constituent principles. And in affirming this He affirmed both the necessity and the possibility to every man of being born exactly as He Himself, as typical man regenerate, is said to have been born, of Virgin Mary and Holy Ghost, and also His own identity in kind with all other men. And He affirmed, moreover, the utter falsity of that priest-constructed system, which, ignoring Regeneration, insists on Substitution, as the means of salvation. For "Virgin Mary," and "Holy Ghost," are but the mystical synonyms with "Water and the Spirit," the substance and force, or soul and spirit, of which, man is constituted, in their divine because pure condition, the product of which in man is the new regenerate selfhood called, as by St Paul, the "Christ within." Begotten in man as matrix, of the pure Spirit and Substance which are God, this new selfhood is son at once of God and of man; and in him God and man are "reconciled" or "at-oned." And that man is said to be saved by his blood, is because the "blood of God" is pure spirit, and it is the pure spirit in the man that saves him; and that he is called the only-begotten Son of God, is not because God begets no other of his kind, but because God, as God, begets directly none of any other kind.

This, then, as we came to learn, and to recognise as having learned it in our own long-past lives, is the doctrine which Jesus came to teach and to demonstrate in His own person. Matter is spirit, being spiritual substance, projected by force of the divine Will into conditions and limitations, and made exteriorly cognisable. And being spirit it can revert to the condition of spirit. In virtue of the divinity of his constituent principles, man has within himself the seed of his own regeneration, and the power to effectuate it. He has in him, this is to say, the potentiality of divinity realisable at will. And the secret and method of the achievement, which is no other than the secret and method of Christ, is inward purification and unfoldment, the unfoldment of the capacities, mental, moral, and spiritual, of his nature, of which inward purification is the first and essential condition. Thus is the Finding of Christ the realisation of the Ideal, and Christ is for every man the summit of his own evolution.

Stated in terms of modern science, but correcting its aberrations, the doctrine of Christ is in this wise. Evolution is the manifestation of inherency. Owing to the divinity of the constituent principles of existence, its Force and its Substance, both of which are God, the inherency of existence is divine. Wherefore, as the manifestation of a divine inherency, evolution is accomplished only by the attainment of divinity; and the cause of evolution is the tendency of substance to revert from its secondary and "created" condition of matter, to its original and divine condition of pure spirit. Wherefore evolution is definable as the process of the individuation of Deity in and through Humanity.

Such is the genesis of the Christ in man. And he is called *a* Christ who, having accomplished this process in himself, returns into the earth-life when he has no need to do so for his own sake, out of pure love to redeem, by showing to others their own equal divine potentialities and the method of the realisation thereof.

This method consists in love, love of perfection, which is God, for its own sake, and love for others. The process is entirely interior to the individual. It consists in the sacrifice of the lower nature to the higher in himself, and of himself for others in love. That which directly saves the man is not the love of another for the man, but the love which he has in himself. All that can be done by another is to kindle this love in him.

The philosophy of this doctrine of salvation by love was formulated for us as follows:—"It is love which is the centripetal power of the universe; it is by love that all creation returns into the bosom of God. The force which projected all things is will, and will is the centrifugal power of the universe. Will alone could not overcome the evil which results from the limitations of matter; but it shall be overcome in the end by sympathy, which is the knowledge of God in others,—the recognition of the omnipresent Self. This is love. And it is with the children of the spirit, the servants of love, that the dragon of matter makes war"[71].

In making the means of salvation extraneous to the individual, Sacerdotalism has defrauded man of his Saviour, making the first and personal coming of Christ of none effect. Hence the necessity for the second and spiritual coming represented by the New Gospel of Interpretation as was foretold:—the coming which was to be in the clouds of the heaven of man's restored understanding; the Hermes within.

But the process of regeneration is a prolonged one, extending over many earth-lives; and so also is the prior process of evolution, whereby man reaches the stage at which he is amenable to regeneration. Wherefore regeneration has for its corollary reincarnation. To tell man that he "must be born again" spiritually, and deny him the requisite opportunities of experience, which must be acquired while in the body—seeing that regeneration is *from out of the body*—would be to mock him.

This doctrine of a multiplicity of earth-lives is implicit and sometimes explicit in the Bible. The notion that the Hebrews had no belief in a future state because of the failure of commentators to discover it in their Scriptures, is altogether futile. The permanence of the Ego was a matter of course with them, saving only the Sadducees. And the Bible contemplates the persistence of the individual soul through all the manifold stages of its evolution, from the "Adam" stage to the "Christ" stage, saying, as by St Paul, "As in Adam all die, so in Christ shall all be made alive." But the Christ insisted on by him was not He Who is "after the flesh," not the man Jesus, who was but the vehicle of the Christ, but the Christ within both Jesus and all other regenerate men. For, as a highly illuminated follower of the Gnosis, St Paul was one who "after the way which" his orthodox accusers "called heresy, worshipped the God of his fathers, believing all things which are according to the law, and are written in the prophets." Rejecting the doctrine of regeneration, and with it that of reincarnation, in favour of substitution, the orthodoxy which claims to be Christianity has practically rejected both the doctrine of St Paul and that of Jesus as declared to Nicodemus. And, as St Paul implies, the "mystery of iniquity" was working even already in his days to annul the gospel of Christ by substituting Jesus as the object of worship, and His physical blood-shedding as the means of salvation. And Christendom, yielding to sacerdotal dictation, has to this day accepted a doctrine which at once dishonours God and robs men of their equal divine potentialities with Jesus, thus preferring Barabbas. Professing to rest its faith on the Bible, it has accepted the presentation of religion which the Bible persistently condemns, that of the priests, and rejected that on which the Bible emphatically insists, that of the prophets. That St Paul employed sacerdotal modes of expression was in order to spiritualise them. He was a mystic of mystics.

Nevertheless the dogmas of the Church contain the truth, but this is not as the Church has propounded them. And—to cite two crucial instances—so far from the Church's supreme dogmas, the Immaculate Conception and the Assumption of the Blessed Virgin, having any personal or physical reference, they are prophecies of the method of redemption for every individual soul. For, as the New Gospel of Interpretation explicitly declares, restoring the Gnosis persistently rejected by the builders of the orthodoxies,The Immaculate Conception is none other than the prophecy of the means whereby the universe shall at last be redeemed. Maria—the sea of limitless space—Maria the Virgin, born herself immaculate and without spot, of the womb of the ages, shall in the fulness of time bring forth the perfect man, who shall redeem the race. He is not one man, but ten thousand times ten thousand, the Son of Man, who shall overcome the limitations of matter, and the evil which is the result of the materialisation of spirit[72].

By the doctrine of the Immaculate Conception of the Blessed Virgin Mary we are secretly enlightened concerning the generation of the soul, who is begotten in the womb of matter, and yet from the first instant of her being is pure and incorrupt.... As the Immaculate Conception is the foundation of the mysteries, so is the Assumption their crown.For the entire object and end of kosmic evolution is precisely this triumph and apotheosis of the soul. In the mystery presented by this dogma, we behold the consummation of the whole scheme of creation—the perpetuation and glorification of the individual human ego. The grave—the material and astral consciousness, cannot retain the immaculate Mother of God. She rises into the heavens; she assumes divinity.... From end to end the mystery of the soul's evolution—the history, that is, of humanity and of the kosmic drama—is contained and enacted in the cultus of the Blessed Virgin Mary. The acts and the glories of Mary are the one supreme subject of the holy mysteries[73]."Allegory of stupendous significance!" exclaimed the seeress's illuminator when imparting to her the mystery of the Immaculate Conception. "Allegory of stupendous significance! with which the Church of God has so long been familiar, but which yet never penetrated its understanding, like the holy fire which enveloped the sacred Bush, but which nevertheless the Bush withstood and resisted[72]."That such failure has been the rule and not the exception is the plea for the New Gospel of Interpretation. For lack of comprehension of its own symbols the Church has fallen into the disastrous errors of mistaking the man Jesus for the Christ within every man, and Mary the mother of Jesus for Virgin Mary the mother of that Christ, committing in both instances idolatry by preferring the form to the substance, persons to principles, and blinding men to the essential truth implied.

CHAPTER VI.
THE EXEMPLIFICATION.

This chapter will be devoted to some examples of the recovered Gnosis, bearing chiefly upon the supreme doctrine of Regeneration. As with all else received by the Seeress, they are the product of intuitional memory regained under divine illumination occurring mostly in sleep. And here I will take occasion to state explicitly and positively, that the states, whether of sleep or of trance, in which her faculty was exercised, were all natural and spontaneous, being induced by the Spirit itself; and that in no case were artificial means employed by either of us, whether drugs, mesmerism, hypnotism, crystal-gazing, or any other of the devices ordinarily used to induce abnormal states of consciousness or promote enhancement of faculty. Our work was to be a real work, done not only by us but in us, and we had from the first a profound instinctive distrust of results obtained by such artificial stimulation.

Nor was any change even of a word ever made in the teachings received. They came one and all in the finished perfection in which they are put forth, coming down as the holy city from the heaven of the upper and the within, and incapable of improvement. The following are the examples proposed:—

(1) Concerning Holy Writ.

All Scriptures which are the true Word of God, have a dual interpretation, the intellectual and the intuitional, the apparent and the hidden.

For nothing can come forth from God save that which is fruitful.

As is the nature of God, so is the Word of God's mouth.

The letter alone is barren; the spirit and the letter give life.

But that Scripture is the more excellent, which is exceeding fruitful and brings forth abundant signification.

For God is able to say many things in one, as the perfect ovary contains many seeds in its chalice.

Therefore there are in the Scriptures of God's Word certain writings which, as richly yielding trees, bear more abundantly than others in the self-same holy garden.

And one of the most excellent is the history of the generation of the heavens and the earth.

For therein is contained in order a genealogy, which has four heads, as a stream divided into four branches, a word exceeding rich.

And the first of these generations is that of the Gods.

The second is that of the kingdom of heaven.

The third is that of the visible world.

And the fourth is that of the Church of Christ.

(2) Concerning the Mystery of Redemption.

All things in heaven and in earth are of God, both the invisible and the visible.

Such as is the invisible, is the visible also, for there is no boundary line betwixt spirit and matter.

Matter is spirit made exteriorly cognisable by the force of the Divine Word.

And when God shall resume all things by love, the material shall be resolved into the spiritual, and there shall be a new heaven and a new earth.

Not that matter shall be destroyed, for it came forth from God, and is of God indestructible and eternal.

But it shall be indrawn and resolved into its true self.

It shall put off corruption, and remain incorruptible.

It shall put off mortality, and remain immortal.

So that nothing be lost of the Divine substance.

It was material entity: it shall be spiritual entity.

For there is nothing which can go out from the presence of God.

This is the doctrine of the resurrection of the dead: that is, the transfiguration of the body.

For the body, which is matter, is but the manifestation of spirit: and the Word of God shall transmute it into its inner being.

The will of God is the alchemic crucible: and the dross which is cast therein is matter.

And the dross shall become pure gold, seven times refined; even perfect spirit.

It shall leave behind it nothing: but shall be transformed into the Divine image.

For it is not a new substance: but its alchemic polarity is changed, and it is converted.

But except it were gold in its true nature, it could not be resumed into the aspect of gold.

And except matter were spirit, it could not revert to spirit.

To make gold, the alchemist must have gold.

But he knows that to be gold which others take to be dross.

Cast thyself into the will of God, and thou shalt become as God.

For thou art God, if thy will be the Divine Will.

This is the great secret: it is the mystery of Redemption.

(3) Concerning Sin and Death.

As is the outer so is the inner: He that worketh is One.

As the small is, so is the great: there is one law.

Nothing is small and nothing is great in the Divine Economy.

If thou wouldst understand the method of the world's corruption, and the condition to which sin hath reduced the work of God,

Meditate upon the aspect of a corpse; and consider the method of the putrefaction of its tissues and humours.

For the secret of death is the same, whether of the outer or of the inner.

The body dieth when the central will of its system no longer bindeth in obedience the elements of its substance.

Every cell is a living entity, whether of vegetable or of animal potency.

In the healthy body every cell is polarised in subjection to the central will, the Adonai of the physical system.

Health, therefore, is order, obedience, and government.

But wherever disease is, there is disunion, rebellion, and insubordination.

And the deeper the seat of the confusion, the more dangerous the malady, and the harder to quell it.

That which is superficial may be more easily healed; or, if need be, the disorderly elements may be rooted out, and the body shall be whole and at unity again.

But if the disobedient molecules corrupt each other continually, and the perversity spread, and the rebellious tracts multiply their elements; the whole body shall fall into dissolution, which is death.

For the central will that should dominate all the kingdom of the body, is no longer obeyed; and every element is become its own ruler, and hath a divergent will of its own.

So that the poles of the cells incline in divers directions; and the binding power which is the life of the body, is dissolved and destroyed.

And when dissolution is complete, then follow corruption and putrefaction.

Now, that which is true of the physical, is true likewise of its prototype.

The whole world is full of revolt; and every element hath a will divergent from God.

Whereas there ought to be but one will, attracting and ruling the whole man.

But there is no longer Brotherhood among you; nor order, nor mutual sustenance.

Every cell is its own arbiter; and every member is become a sect.

Ye are not bound one to another: ye have confounded your offices, and abandoned your functions.

Ye have reversed the direction of your magnetic currents: ye are fallen into confusion, and have given place to the spirit of misrule.

Your wills are many and diverse; and every one of you is an anarchy.

A house that is divided against itself, falleth.

O wretched man; who shall deliver you from this body of Death?

(4) Concerning the Twelve Gates of Regeneration.

Now, the Kingdom of God is within us; that is, it is interior, invisible, mystic, spiritual.

There is a power by means of which the Outer may be absorbed into the Inner.

There is a power by means of which Matter may be ingested into its original Substance.

He who possesses this power is Christ, and He has the devil under foot.

For He reduces chaos to order, and indraws the external to the centre.

He has learnt that Matter is illusion, and that Spirit alone is real.

He has found His own Central Point; and all power is given unto Him in heaven and on earth.

Now, the Central Point is the number Thirteen: it is the number of the Marriage of the Son of God.

And all the members of the microcosm are bidden to the banquet of the marriage.

But if there chance to be even one among them which has not on a wedding garment,

Such a one is a Traitor, and the microcosm is found divided against itself.

And that it may be wholly regenerate, it is necessary that Judas be cast out.

Now the members of the microcosm are Twelve: of the Senses three, of the Mind three, of the Heart three, and of the Conscience three.

For of the Body there are four elements; and the sign of the four is Sense, in the which are three Gates,

The gate of the Eye, the gate of the Ear, and the gate of the Touch[74].

Renounce vanity, and be poor: renounce praise, and be humble: renounce luxury, and be chaste.

Offer unto God a pure oblation: let the fire of the altar search thee, and prove thy fortitude.

Cleanse thy sight, thine hands, and thy feet: carry the censer of thy worship into the courts of the Lord; and let thy vows be unto the Most High.

And for the magnetic man[75] there are four elements: and the covering of the four is mind, in the which are three gates;

The gate of desire, the gate of labour, and the gate of illumination.

Renounce the world, and aspire heavenward: labour not for the meat which perishes, but ask of God thy daily bread: beware of wandering doctrines, and let the Word of the Lord be thy light.

Also of the soul there are four elements: and the seat of the four is the heart, whereof likewise there are three gates;

The gate of obedience, the gate of prayer, and the gate of discernment.

Renounce thine own will, and let the law of God only be within thee: renounce doubt: pray always and faint not: be pure of heart also, and thou shalt see God.

And within the soul is the Spirit: and the Spirit is One, yet has it likewise three elements.

And these are the gates of the oracle of God, which is the ark of the covenant;

The rod, the host[76], and the law:

The force which solves, and transmutes, and divines: the bread of heaven which is the substance of all things and the food of angels; the table of the law, which is the will of God, written with the finger of the Lord.

If these three be within thy spirit, then shall the Spirit of God be within thee.

And the glory shall be upon the propitiatory, in the holy place of thy prayer.

These are the twelve gates of regeneration: through which if a man enter he shall have right to the tree of life.

For the number of that Tree is Thirteen.

It may happen to a man to have three, to another five, to another seven, to another ten.

But until a man have twelve, he is not master over the last enemy.

(5) Concerning the Passage of the Soul[77].

Evoi, Father Iacchos, Lord God of Egypt: initiate thy servants in the halls of thy Temple;

Upon whose walls are the forms of every creature: of every beast of the earth, and of every fowl of the air;

The lynx, and the lion, and the bull: the ibis and the serpent: the scorpion and every flying thing.

And the columns thereof are human shapes; having the heads of eagles and the hoofs of the ox.

All these are of thy kingdom: they are the chambers of ordeal, and the houses of the initiation of the soul.

For the soul passeth from form to form; and the mansions of her pilgrimage are manifold.

Thou callest her from the deep, and from the secret places of the earth; from the dust of the ground, and from the herb of the field.

Thou coverest her nakedness with an apron of fig-leaves; thou clothest her with the skins of beasts.

Thou art from of old, O soul of man; yea, thou art from the everlasting.

Thou puttest off thy bodies as raiment; and as vesture dost thou fold them up.

They perish, but thou remainest: the wind rendeth and scattereth them; and the place of them shall no more be known.

For the wind is the Spirit of God in man, which bloweth where it listeth, and thou hearest the sound thereof, but canst not tell whence it cometh, nor whither it shall go.

Even so is the spirit of man, which cometh from afar off and tarrieth not, but passeth away to a place thou knowest not.

(6) Concerning the Mystic Exodus[77].

Evoi, Iacchos, Lord of the Sphinx; who linkest the lowest to the highest; the loins of the wild beast to the head and breast of the woman.

Thou holdest the chalice of divination: all the forms of nature are reflected therein.

Thou turnest man to destruction: then thou sayest, Come again, ye children of my hand.

Yea, blessed and holy art thou, O Master of Earth: Lord of the cross and the tree of salvation.

Vine of God, whose blood redeemeth; bread of heaven, broken on the altar of death.

There is corn in Egypt; go thou down into her, O my soul, with joy.

For in the kingdom of the Body, thou shalt eat the bread of thine initiation.

But beware lest thou become subject to the flesh, and a bond-slave in the land of thy sojourn.

Serve not the idols of Egypt; and let not the senses be thy taskmasters.

For they will bow thy neck to their yoke; they will bitterly oppress the Israel of God.

An evil time shall come upon thee; and the Lord shall smite Egypt with plagues for thy sake.

Thy body shall be broken on the wheel of God; thy flesh shall see trouble and the worm.

Thy house shall be smitten with grievous plagues; blood, and pestilence, and great darkness; fire shall devour thy goods; and thou shalt be a prey to the locust and creeping thing.

Thy glory shall be brought down to the dust; hail and storm shall smite thine harvest; yea, thy beloved and thy first-born shall the hand of the Lord destroy;

Until the body let the soul go free; that she may serve the Lord God.

Arise in the night, O soul, and fly, lest thou be consumed in Egypt.

The angel of the understanding shall know thee for his elect, if thou offer unto God a reasonable faith.

Savour thy reason with learning, with labour, and with obedience.

Let the rod of thy desire be in thy right hand: put the sandals of Hermes on thy feet; and gird thy loins with strength.

Then shalt thou pass through the waters of cleansing, which is the first death in the body.

The waters shall be a wall unto thee on thy right hand and on thy left.

And Hermes the Redeemer shall go before thee; for he is thy cloud of darkness by day, and thy pillar of fire by night.

All the horsemen of Egypt and the chariots thereof; her princes, her counsellors, and her mighty men:

These shall pursue thee, O soul, that fliest; and shall seek to bring thee back into bondage.

Fly for thy life; fear not the deep; stretch out thy rod over the sea; and lift thy desire unto God.

Thou hast learnt wisdom in Egypt; thou has spoiled the Egyptians; thou hast carried away their fine gold and their precious things.

Thou hast enriched thyself in the body; but the body shall not hold thee; neither shall the waters of the deep swallow thee up.

Thou shalt wash thy robes in the sea of regeneration; the blood of atonement shall redeem thee to God.

This is thy chrism and anointing, O soul; this is the first death; thou art the Israel of the Lord,

Who hath redeemed thee from the dominion of the body; and hath called thee from the grave, and from the house of bondage,

Unto the way of the cross, and to the path in the midst of the wilderness;

Where are the adder and the serpent, the mirage and the burning sand.

For the feet of the saint are set in the way of the desert.

But be thou of good courage, and fail thou not; then shall thy raiment endure, and thy sandals shall not wax old upon thee.

And thy desire shall heal thy diseases; it shall bring streams for thee out of the stony rock; it shall lead thee to Paradise.

Evoi, Father Iacchos, Jehovah-Nissi[78]; Lord of the garden and of the vineyard;

Initiator and lawgiver; God of the cloud and of the mount.

Evoi, Father Iacchos; out of Egypt has thou called thy Son.

To vindicate the suppressed mysteries of the pre-Christian churches by disclosing them as the true *origines* of Christianity, and to replace the false doctrine of the exclusive divinity of one man by the true doctrine of the potential divinity of all men,—these are among the foremost objects of the New Gospel of Interpretation. And it is especially in order to reinforce the last named, that it has restored the following hymn in celebration of the supreme results of regeneration, which formed part of the ritual of the greater mysteries of the Greeks. It is addressed to the first of the Holy Seven, the Spirit of Wisdom, as represented by his "angel," the angel of the sun, even "that light which Adonai created on the first day," "whose name is, in the Hebrew, Uriel, and in the Greek, Phoibos, the Bright One of God." Breathing both the Spirit and the letter of the Bible, from Genesis to the Apocalypse, the hymns, of which this is one, indicate unmistakeably the identity in source and substance of the Hebrew and the Christian with the other sacred mysteries of antiquity, and the derivation of the later through the earlier from their common source in the world celestial when once again they have been restored. And they supply also the motive which led the Christians to destroy the second Alexandrian library, showing that motive to have been the desire to conceal, first, the derivation of the

Christian presentment from its predecessors, and next, the perversion of their doctrine in the interests of an unscrupulous sacerdocy.

Taken in connection with its fellow-hymns, similarly recovered, to others of the "Holy Seven," the hymn to Phoibos throws a flood of light on the creative week of Genesis, showing it to be no mere proem to Scripture, or concerned with the world physical merely, but an integral portion of Scripture, being an epitome of eternal verities ever in process, and appertaining both to Creation and to Redemption. The Hymn to Her who is mystically the fourth, but really the third of the Gods, the "Spirit of Counsel" of Isaiah, is especially notable for its solution of the problem of the inversion of the order of the third and fourth days of creation. These hymns, moreover, show indubitably that the order of the solar system was no secret to the hierophants of the sacred mysteries of antiquity.

(7) Hymn to Phoibos, the First of the Gods.

"Strong art thou and adorable, Phoibos Apollo, who bearest life and healing on thy wings, who crownest the year with thy bounty, and givest the spirit of thy divinity to the fruits and precious things of all the worlds.

Where were the bread of the initiation of the Sons of God, except thou bring the corn to ear; or the wine of their mystical chalice, except thou bless the vintage?

Many are the angels who serve in the courts of the spheres of heaven: but thou, Master of Light and of Life, art followed by the Christs of God.

And thy sign is the sign of the Son of Man in heaven, and of the Just made perfect;

Whose path is as a shining light, shining more and more unto the innermost glory of the day of the Lord God.

Thy banner is blood-red, and thy symbol is a milk-white lamb, and thy crown is of pure gold.

They who reign with thee are the Hierophants of the celestial mysteries; for their will is the will of God, and they know as they are known.

These are the sons of the innermost sphere; the Saviours of men, the Anointed of God.

And their name is Christ Jesus, in the day of their initiation.

And before them every knee shall bow, of things in heaven and of things on earth.

They are come out of great tribulation, and are set down for ever at the right hand of God.

And the Lamb, which is in the midst of the seven spheres, shall give them to drink of the river of living water.

And they shall eat of the tree of life, which is in the centre of the garden of the kingdom of God.

These are thine, O Mighty Master of Light; and this is the dominion which the Word of God appointed thee in the beginning:

In the day when God created the light of all the worlds, and divided the light from the darkness.

And God called the light Phoibos, and the darkness God called Python.

Now the darkness was before the light, as the night forerunneth the dawn.

These are the evening and the morning of the first cycle of the Mysteries.

And the glory of that cycle is as the glory of seven days; and they who dwell therein are seven times refined;

Who have purged the garment of the flesh in the living waters;

And have transmuted both body and soul into spirit, and are become pure virgins.

For they were constrained by love to abandon the outer elements, and to seek the innermost which is undivided, even the Wisdom of God.

And wisdom and love are one.

In view of the restoration of the Gods to recognition by the New Gospel of Interpretation, it must be explained that the doctrines of Monotheism and Polytheism are not necessarily incompatible. This has already been shown in Chapter IV., in the utterance commencing—"In the bosom of the Eternal were all the Gods comprehended, as the seven spirits of the prism contained in the Invisible Light." For as light is one though its rays are seven and each ray is light, so is God one though His spirits are seven and each spirit is God.

And yet further. The deities recognised under various names or by various peoples are not necessarily different Gods, but may be either the same God or different modes or aspects of the same God. Notably is this the case with the Gods of the Hebrews, the Greeks, and the Christians. For while by the term Elohim is denoted the two principles, masculine and feminine, of Force and Substance, which constitute Original Being, by Jehovah or Yahveh, Adonai and Shaddai, is denoted the resultant of the interaction of these two principles as Father and Mother, who is called therefore their word, expression, and Son. By the Holy Ghost is denoted the same two principles in activity, having procession from the "Father-Mother" through the "Son," to be the constituent principles of creation, being Deity dynamic as distinguished from Deity static. By the Seven Spirits of God—as by the seven great Gods of the Greeks,—are denoted the seven potencies into which Deity differentiates on emerging as Holy Ghost from the prism constituted of Father, Mother, and Son, which are to each other as the force, substance, and phenomenon of which every manifest entity consists. For "Every entity that is manifest, is manifest by the evolution of its trinity." And by Christ is denoted the ultimate issue of such procession of Deity into manifestation, namely, divinity individuated by means of its passage through matter, and elaborated by co-operation of the Seven Spirits of God, into a perfected *spiritual* Ego, who is at once God and man, and subsists under two modes—the microcosmic or individual, and the macrocosmic or universal, and who is always in process of increase, because, in manifestation, "the Father is greater than the Son;" and "the manifest never exhausts the unmanifest."

Now the process of the Christ is by regeneration, and of this, as has been said, reincarnation is the condition. The New Gospel of Interpretation contains an utterance of Jesus on this subject which will fitly conclude this series of examples. It was recovered by "Mary" under illumination early in 1880, and consequently when we had not fully come to realise the actuality of the doctrine and the possibility of the recovery of the memories of past lives. Hence she sought from her illuminators confirmation of the genuineness of the experience, when she was distinctly and positively assured that the incident had actually occurred, and that she had borne part in it, though no record of it survives. Such is the extrinsic testimony on which it rests. We found the intrinsic no less satisfactory, whether as regards the substance or the form.

(8) Concerning the previous lines of Jesus, and Reincarnation.

This morning between sleeping and waking I saw myself, together with many other persons, walking with Jesus in the fields round about Jerusalem, and while He was speaking to us, a man approached, who looked very earnestly upon Him. And Jesus turned to us and said, "This man whom you see approaching is a seer. He can behold the past lives of a man by looking into his face." Then, the man being come up to us, Jesus took him by the hand and said, "What readest thou?" And the man answered, "I see Thy past, Lord Jesus, and the ways by which Thou hast come." And Jesus said to him, "Say on." So the man told Jesus that he could see Him in the past for many long ages back. But of all that he named, I remember but one incarnation, or, perhaps, one only struck me, and that was *Isaac*. And as the man went on speaking, and enumerating the incarnations he saw, Jesus waved His right hand twice or thrice before his eyes, and said, "It is enough," as though He wished him not to reveal further. Then I stepped forward from the rest and said, "Lord, if, as thou hast taught us, the woman is the highest form of humanity, and the last to be assumed, how comes it that Thou, the Christ, art still in the lower form of man? Why comest Thou not to lead the perfect life, and to save the world as woman? For surely Thou has attained to womanhood." And Jesus answered, "I have attained to womanhood, as thou sayest; and already have I taken the form of woman. But there are three conditions under which the soul returns to the man's form; and they are these:—

"1st. When the work which the Spirit proposes to accomplish is of a nature unsuitable to the female form.

"2nd. When the Spirit has failed to acquire, in the degree necessary to perfection, certain special attributes of the male character.

"3rd. When the Spirit has transgressed, and gone back in the path of perfection, by degrading the womanhood it had attained.

"In the first of these cases the return to the male form is outward and superficial only. This is my case. I am a woman in all save the body. But had My body been a woman's, I could not have led the life necessary to the work I have to perform. I could not have trod the rough ways of the earth, nor have gone about from city to city preaching, nor have fasted on the mountains, nor have fulfilled My mission of poverty and labour. Therefore am I—a woman—clothed in a man's body that I may be enabled to do the work set before Me.

"The second case is that of a soul who, having been a woman perhaps many times, has acquired more aptly and readily the higher qualities of womanhood than the lower qualities of manhood. Such a soul is lacking in energy, in resoluteness, in that particular attribute of the Spirit which the prophet ascribes to the Lord when he says, 'The Lord is a Man of war.' Therefore the soul is put back into a man's form to acquire the qualities yet lacking.

"The third case is that of the backslider, who, having nearly attained perfection,—perhaps even touched it,—degrades and soils his white robe, and is put back into the lower form again. These are the common cases; for there are few women who are worthy to be women"[79].

(9) Concerning the "Work of Power."

You have asked me if the Work of Power is a difficult one, and if it is open to all.

It is open to all potentially and eventually, but not actually and in the present. In order to regain power and the resurrection, a man must be a Hierarch; that is to say, he must have attained the *magical* age of thirty-three. This age is attained by having accomplished the Twelve Labours, passed the Twelve Gates, overcome the Five Senses, and obtained dominion over the Four Spirits of the elements. He must have been born Immaculate, baptised with Water and Fire, tempted in the Wilderness, crucified and buried. He must have borne Five Wounds on the Cross, and he must have answered the riddle of the Sphinx. When this is accomplished he is free of matter, and will never again have a phenomenal body.

Who shall attain to this perfection? The Man who is without fear and without concupiscence; who has courage to be absolutely poor and absolutely chaste. When it is all one to you whether you have gold or whether you have none, whether you have a house and lands or whether you have them not, whether you have worldly reputation or whether you are an outcast,—then you are voluntarily poor. It is not necessary to have nothing, but it is necessary to care for nothing. When it is all one to you whether you have a wife or husband, or whether you are celibate, then you are free from concupiscence. It is not necessary to be a virgin; it is necessary to set no value on the flesh. There is nothing so difficult to attain as this equilibrium. Who is he who can part with his goods without regret? Who is he who is never consumed by the desires of the flesh? But when you have ceased both to wish to retain and to burn, then you have the remedy in your own hands, and the remedy is a hard and a sharp one, and a terrible ordeal. Nevertheless, be not afraid. Deny the five senses, and above all the taste and the touch. The power is within you if you will to attain it. The Two Seats are vacant at the Celestial Table, if you will put on Christ. Eat no dead thing. Drink no fermented drink. Make living elements of all the elements of your body. Mortify the members of earth. Take your food full of life, and let not the touch of death pass upon it. You understand me, but you shrink. Remember that without self-immolation, there is no power over death. Deny the touch. Seek no bodily pleasure in sexual communion; let desire be magnetic and soulic. If you indulge the body, you perpetuate the body, and the end of the body is corruption. You understand me again, but you shrink. Remember that without self-denial and restraint there is no power over death. Deny the taste first, and it will become easier to deny the touch. For to be a virgin is the crown of discipline. I have shown you the excellent way, and it is the *Via Dolorosa*. Judge whether the resurrection be worth the passion; whether the kingdom be worth the obedience; whether the power be worth the suffering. When the time of your calling comes, you will no longer hesitate.

When a man has attained power over his body, the process of ordeal is no longer necessary. The Initiate is under a vow; the Hierarch is free. Jesus, therefore, came eating and drinking; for all things were lawful to Him. He had undergone, and had freed His will. For the object of the trial and the vow is polarisation. When the fixed is volatilised, the Magian is free. But before Christ was Christ He was subject; and His initiation lasted thirty years. All things are lawful to the Hierarch; for he knows the nature and value of all[89].

This chapter may appropriately terminate with a few remarks in reply to the inevitable question, why our country and language were selected as the place and tongue of the new revelation in preference to all others.

It is, as we were enabled to see, because the British people are recognised in the celestial world, as possessing that peculiar quality of soul which, in spite of their many and grievous limitations, has made them to be the foremost witness among the nations to God and the Conscience, in such wise as to constitute them the counterpart of Israel in the modern world. Others besides ourselves have recognised this characteristic. Said Milton, speaking of a crisis which, momentous as it was, pales in presence of that which now is, seeing that Religion itself as Religion was not menaced then as in our time—"Now once again, by all concurrence of signs, and by the general instinct of devout and holy men, as they daily and solemnly express their thoughts, God is beginning to devise some new and great period in His Church, even to the reforming of Reformation itself. What does He then, but address Himself to His servants, and—as His manner is—first to His Englishmen."

To which we may add in reference to the present, "And having by the hands of His Intellectualists, beaten down the false interpretation of His holy Word, accomplishing the work of destruction, is about by the hands of His Intuitionalists, to establish the true interpretation, accomplishing the work of re-construction." Nor are there wanting specific historical facts pointing in the same direction. To Britain it was given by a timely act of revolt against a domination at once foreign and sacerdotal, to rescue the letter of Scripture from suppression and virtual extinction at the hands of an order bent only on exalting itself at whatever cost to truth and humanity. Meanwhile, for three centuries and a half—period suggestive of the mystical "time, times, and half a time,"—Britain has faithfully and lovingly, albeit unintelligently and mistakenly, guarded and cherished the letter thus rescued, even to the erecting of it into a fetish. And it may well be that she has now, for her guerdon, been further commissioned to be the recipient and minister of its interpretation.Moreover, as Mistress of the Sea, the especial symbol of the Soul, she has a prescriptive claim to be the vehicle of the latest and crowning message to earth, of which the Soul herself is at once the source, the subject, and the object.Nor are the universality of her language and the grandeur of her literature elements to be left out of consideration. All things point to her language as destined to become, practically, the language of the world; and hence its peculiar fitness to be the vehicle of that "eternal gospel" which it is declared should, at the end of the age, be proclaimed "unto them that dwell on the earth, even unto every nation, and tribe, and tongue, and people."

CHAPTER VII.
THE PROMULGATION AND RECOGNITION.

As will readily be imagined, the interest was intense with which we watched the progress of our work, in order to see whether the crucial event of its promulgation would coincide with the date prophesied for the turning point between the outgoing and the incoming dispensations. The predictions covered a period of six years, namely from 1876 to 1881 inclusive. In this period was to be laid the foundation of a universal kingdom of justice and knowledge, which should constitute the reign of Michael, and spring from a new illumination, one feature of which was to be the "return of the Gods" in 1876. It was in the autumn of this year that they first came to us, and the intimation was given us that the reign of Michael was then actually commencing; we having no knowledge either of the meaning or of the fact of such predictions. For, while the Bible references to Michael were altogether unintelligible to us, we had not learnt to refer the event to any assignable period. The fulfilment of this prediction disposed us to attach value to those which pointed to the year 1881 as that in which our work—supposing our estimate of its significance to be correct—ought to see the light. For our illuminators observed silence respecting times and seasons, contenting themselves with bringing under our notice the books containing the predictions, the application being left to our own perspicacity. We were powerless to influence events, even had we desired to do so. We could but work steadily on, as we did, "without haste, without rest," until my colleague had finished her university course and obtained her diploma. This she accomplished in the summer of 1880, soon after which we returned to England; and in the summer of 1881 we delivered in London, to a private audience, the lectures which constituted the first promulgation of our work. These were published in the following winter under the title of "The Perfect Way, or the Finding of Christ," our excellent friend at Paris faithfully fulfilling the mission she had accepted in relation to us and our work[81]. Thus were fulfilled exactly all the predictions respecting the dates, the character, and the manner of our work.

There were many other coincidences of a kind so remarkable as to make us feel that to ascribe them to accident would require a larger measure of credulity than to ascribe them to design. Among the most striking were those which concerned "Mary's" names, and which were in this wise.

When first the significance of the Apocalyptic utterance concerning the river Euphrates and the kings of the East was flashed on my mind, I asked her if she knew that she was mentioned, even to her very name, in the book of Revelation. To which she replied, smiling, that she had known it for some time, but which of her names did I mean? I said that I meant her married surname, which fitted exactly a way made for kings across a river, by the drying up of its waters, namely a *king's ford*; the "Kings of the East," meaning those principles in man whereby he has knowledge of divine things—the East being the mystical expression for the place of the dawn of spiritual light, such as that of which she was the revealer. While the Euphrates means, in the Apocalypse as in Genesis, the highest principle in the fourfold kosmos of man, the Spirit or Will[82]. Only when this principle in man is "dried up," or sublimated by being made one with the divine Will, is man accessible to the divine knowledges brought by the "Kings of the East." As the channel by which these knowledges were being restored to the world, she was the *kings' ford* implied. She then told me, what I had not yet observed, that her baptismal and maiden names were equally appropriate, as the Latin for the "acceptable year of the Lord," or *good time*, announced as to follow the restoration of the knowledges brought by the Kings of the East, is—allowing for difference of gender—*Annus Bonus*. The coincidence of names did not end here, for we shortly afterwards, in the course of our researches, came upon an old prophecy declaring that the initials of the "Messenger" of the new Avâtar, due at this time, would be A. K.!

She further identified the "Kings of the East" as functions of the three principles in man, the Spirit, the Soul, and the Mind; being respectively, right aspiration, which is of the Spirit; right perception, which is of the Soul; and right judgment, which is of the Mind; the combination of which is the necessary and sufficient condition of divine knowledge.

Had we been sanguine of a favourable reception of our book by the press at large—which we were not—our disappointment would have been great. But we were by no means prepared either for the gross misrepresentation and even vulgar ribaldry with which it was treated by the few organs in the literary press which noticed it at all, or for the complete neglect of it by that portion of the press which especially concerns itself with religious exegesis. In no instance was any attempt made to exhibit its plan, purpose, and real nature, or any recognition accorded to its luminous solutions of the profound problems dealt with. The very claim to have experiential knowledge of things spiritual was accounted an offence; and it seemed as if the word had gone forth to adopt towards it an attitude which should effectually restrain the public from making its acquaintance, even though it met absolutely the need recognised on all hands as the world's supreme need, and vindicated its claim thereto by the presentation of teachings avowedly of divine derivation and demonstrating their divinity by their intrinsic character to all who are in the smallest degree spiritually percipient. To this day that attitude has never been abandoned or relaxed; and notwithstanding the assiduous endeavours made to counteract its influence, the whole mass of our people, saving only a few select circles, have yet to learn that the longed-for New Gospel of Interpretation has actually been vouchsafed, having been for years in their midst waiting but to be recognised of them,—a "light shining in darkness and the darkness comprehending it not"[83].

In compliance with the injunctions of our illuminators, we had withheld our names from our first edition, in order to secure for it a judgment unbiased by any personal element. But though we ourselves thus escaped the opprobrium attaching to our book, "Mary" was at first inclined to repent of having exposed her pearls to such profanation; and was only reassured by the suggestion that it showed how desperate was the need for precisely the change our work was designed to accomplish, and how exactly was fulfilled the prophecy which foretold the wrath of the dragon and his angels at the advent of the "Woman" Intuition, their destined destroyer, and the consequent shortness of their own time. We knew of course better than to regard such criticism as being in any sense a measure of our work. For us it was, like criticism in general, a measure not of the thing criticised but of the critics themselves. And these, in our case, but truly represented the condition of the age, and knew not what they were doing.

Such is the reason why so many will hear for the first time from this book that a New Gospel of Interpretation has been received. To turn to the other and compensating side. With those who were specially qualified to judge, it was far otherwise. And among the most notable of the recognitions received from this quarter was the weighty utterance which appears in the preface to the second and succeeding editions, coming from that veteran student of the "Divine Science," the friend, disciple, and literary heir of the renowned Kabalist and magian, the late Abbé Constant ("Eliphas Levi"), namely, Baron Spedalieri of Marseilles, who though then an entire stranger to us, wrote to us as follows—for I think it may with advantage be reproduced here:—

"As with the corresponding Scriptures of the past, the appeal on behalf of your book is, really, to miracles, but with the difference that in your case they are intellectual ones, and incapable of simulation, being miracles of interpretation. And they have the further distinction of doing no violence to common sense by infringing the possibilities of Nature; while they are in complete accord with all mystical traditions, and especially with the great Mother of these, the Kabala. That miracles such as I am describing are to be found in *The Perfect Way*, in kind and number unexampled, they who are the best qualified to judge will be the most ready to affirm.

"And here, *apropos* of these renowned Scriptures, permit me to offer you some remarks on the Kabala as we have it. It is my opinion—

"(1) That this tradition is far from being genuine, and such as it was on its original emergence from the sanctuaries.

"(2) That when Guillaume Postel—of excellent memory—and his brother Hermetists of the later middle age—the Abbot Trithemius and others—predicted that these sacred books of the Hebrews should become known and understood at the end of the era, and specified the present time for that event, they did not mean that such knowledge should be limited to the mere divulgement of these particular Scriptures, but that it would have for its base a new illumination, which should eliminate from them all that has been ignorantly or wilfully introduced, and should re-unite that great tradition with its source by restoring it in all its purity.

"(3) That this illumination has just been accomplished, and has been manifested in *The Perfect Way*. For in this book we find all that there is of truth in the Kabala, supplemented by new intuitions, such as present a body of doctrine at once complete, homogeneous, logical and inexpungnable.

"Since the whole tradition thus finds itself recovered or restored to its original purity, the prophecies of Postel and his fellow-Hermetists are accomplished; and I consider that from henceforth the study of the Kabala will be but an object of curiosity and erudition, like that of Hebrew antiquities.

"Humanity has always and everywhere asked itself these three supreme questions: Whence come we? What are we? Whither go we? Now, these questions at length find an answer, complete, satisfactory, and consolatory, in *The Perfect Way*"[84].

He subsequently wrote:—

"If the Scriptures of the future are to be, as I firmly believe they will be, those which best interpret the Scriptures of the past, these writings will assuredly hold the foremost place among them"[85].

For those who are unacquainted with the Kabala, its origin, nature, and intent, it will be well to state that it represents the transcendental and esoteric doctrine of the Hebrews, as handed down from the remotest times. In recognition of its divine origin, the Rabbins describe it as having been communicated by God, first, to "Adam in Paradise," and, next, to "Moses on Sinai." By which expressions they implied that its doctrine was due to the highest possible illumination.

It was also in recognition of this element in our book that Mr. MacGregor Mathers dedicated his learned work, "The Kabala Unveiled," to us, saying—

"I have much pleasure in dedicating this work to the authors of *The Perfect Way*, as they have in that excellent and wonderful book touched so much on the doctrines of the Kabala, and laid such value on its teachings. *The Perfect Way* is one of the most deeply occult works that has been written for centuries."

As the foregoing testimonies represent the *consensus* of the Kabalists, Hermetists, and other great ancient schools of spiritual science in the West, so the following represents the *consensus* of the corresponding schools of the East. As will be seen, it involves a coincidence so notable as to point to a source transcending the human and terrestrial, as that of the great spiritual revival which our age is witnessing. That coincidence is in this wise:—

Within two years of the commencement of our collaboration in the work which proved to be that of the restoration of the *Gnosis* of the West—the divine doctrine of which, as we had come to learn, Christ was the personal demonstration, and the religion called after Him ought to have been the expression; a collaboration was commenced which had for its end the like exposition in regard to the religious systems of the East. This is the collaboration, also of a woman and a man, which had its issue in the Theosophical Society. The two pairs of collaborators worked simultaneously through the succeeding years in entire ignorance of each other and their work, until the commencement of the publication of our results in 1881, at which time the Theosophical Society was still so far from having completed the system of its doctrine, that neither of its two now fundamental tenets had yet been recognised by it, the tenets, namely, of Reincarnation and Karma—its chief text-book, the "Isis Unveiled" of its foundress, not containing them. We, on the contrary, had both of these doctrines, having derived them, as already stated herein, directly from celestial sources and wholly independently of human authority and tradition, of spiritualism, and of our own prepossessions.

It was clear, both by this fact and by the avowals of the parties concerned, that up to this time the chiefs of the Theosophical Society had been unable to obtain from those whom they claimed as their masters more than a very meagre instalment of their doctrine. But after the arrival of our book in India this state of things was changed. It was then declared on behalf of the "masters" that we had obtained, from original and independent sources, a system of doctrine substantially identical with that of which they had for ages been, as they supposed, in exclusive possession, but had never been permitted to divulge, as it had always been reserved for initiates. The revelation of it through us, we were further informed, had "forced the hands of the masters," by showing them that the time had come when secrecy was no longer possible, and compelling them, if only in vindication of their own claims, to relax their rule of silence in regard to their mysteries.

The coincidence between their doctrine and ours comprised sundry particulars the most recondite, including—besides the two great tenets already named—the multiplicity of principles in the human system, and their separation and respective conditions after death,—a subject lying outside the cognisance of "Spiritualism." Among other points of agreement was that of their recognition of the great antiquity of the soul of "Mary," whom they pronounced to be "the greatest natural mystic of the present day, and countless ages ahead of the great majority of mankind, the foremost of whom—the most civilised—belong to the last race of the fourth round, while she belongs to the first race of the fifth round."

In presence of these and other proofs of the possession by the Eastern occultists, of knowledges which we had obtained directly at first hand from celestial sources, we could not but pay respectful heed to the claims of the representatives of the Theosophical Society, and welcome any token which might indicate it as a destined fellow-agent in the great spiritual revival of the age. So might it constitute, with "Spiritualism" and the work represented by us, a threefold power for accomplishing the promotion predicted for this era, of the consciousness of the race to a level which should transcend any yet reached by it as a race. With Spiritualism to represent the phenomenal and personal, Theosophy the philosophical and occult, and our own work the mystical and divine, every region of man's higher nature would find its due recognition and unfoldment. Meanwhile, the organ of the Society in India thus expressed itself respecting "The Perfect Way":—

"A grand book, keen of insight and eloquent in exposition; an upheaval of true spirituality.... We regard its authors as having produced one of the most—perhaps the most—important and spirit-stirring of appeals to the highest instincts of mankind which modern European literature has evolved"[86].

We had a yet further warrant, derived from Scripture itself, for looking to the Theosophical Society as possibly a divinely appointed factor in the spiritual evolution of the time. The unsealing of the World's Bibles was upon us, and not of that of Christendom only. And we saw in the following saying of Jesus an obvious allusion to the present epoch, "In those days many shall come from the East, and the West, and the North, and the South, and shall sit down with Abraham, Isaac, and Jacob, in the kingdom of heaven." Not that the terms East, West, North, and South, denoted for us the quarters of the physical globe. We had learnt to understand them in their mystical sense, wherein they denote the various human temperaments, the intuitional, the traditional, the intellectual, and the emotional, all of which would find satisfaction in the doctrine then to be recovered. It was in the terms Abraham, Isaac, and Jacob, that the significance of the utterance lay for us; these being in one aspect the Hebrew equivalents for Brahma, Isis, and Iacchos, and denoting the mysteries respectively of India, Egypt, and Greece, of the Spirit, the Soul, and the Body, and therein of the whole Man. For these mysteries together comprised the perfect doctrine of Existence, called also in Scripture the "Word of God," the "Law and the Prophets," and the "*Theou Sophia*," "Wisdom of God," and "hidden Wisdom," of which the Christ, as the typical Man regenerate, is the fulfilment and personal demonstration. This is to say, they constituted that Gnosis, or Knowledge, with the taking away and withholdment of the key of which Jesus so bitterly reproached, in the Ecclesiasticism of His time, that of all time, and, therefore, that knowledge to the restoration of which, in our day, through the faculty by means of which it was originally obtained and can alone be discerned, the prophecies one and all pointed, as to mark and to make the "time of the end" of the "adulterous," because idolatrous, "generation," hitherto in possession in the Church, and to introduce the "kingdom of God with power."

Having warrant so high for anticipating the restoration at this time of the faculties and knowledges represented by the various movements in question, and knowing also, if only by the example of ourselves, that the divinity of a mission is not invalidated by the limitations, real or supposed, of its instruments, but that these must be educated by experience, and in such sense "perfected through suffering" to be fitted for their appointed tasks;—we had no doubt as to the attitude it was our duty to maintain towards all candidates for a share in that which we recognised as the greatest of all the endeavours yet made by the human soul to regain her long-lost rightful dominion over the minds and hearts of men, leaving it to time to determine that which was of divine appointment, and that which was not.

It will have been observed that I have used the terms "mystical" and "occult" in such wise as to imply a distinction between them. It is important to the purpose of this book to define and emphasise that distinction. The instructions received by us from our illuminators were explicit and positive on this point.

This is because they refer to two different domains of man's system. Occultism deals with transcendental physics, and is of the intellectual, belonging to science. Mysticism deals with transcendental metaphysics, and is of the spiritual, belonging to religion. Occultism, therefore, has for its domain the region which, lying between the body and the soul, is interior to the body but exterior to the soul; while Mysticism has for its domain the region which, comprising the soul and the spirit, is interior to the soul, and belongs to the divine. Of course, the terms themselves, which are respectively the Latin and the Greek for the same thing, and mean hidden from the outer senses and also from non-initiates, do not imply such distinction, but they have come by usage to be thus referable.

The following citations are from the teachings received by us in this connection. They account for the scientific part of the training imposed on us.

"The science of the Mysteries can be understood only by one who has studied the physical sciences, because it is the climax and crown of all these, and must be learned last and not first. Unless thou understand the physical sciences, thou canst not comprehend the doctrine of *Vehicles*, which is the basic doctrine of occult science. 'If thou understood not earthly things, how shall I make thee understand heavenly things?' Wherefore, get knowledge, and be greedy of knowledge, ever more and more. It is idle for thee to seek the inner chamber, until thou hast passed through the outer. This, also, is another reason why occult science cannot be unveiled to the horde. To the unlearned no truth can be demonstrated. Theosophy is the royal science[87]; if thou would reach the king's presence chamber, there is no way save through the outer rooms and galleries of the palace[88].

"The adept or occultist is, at best, a religious scientist; he is not a 'saint.' If occultism were all, and held the key of heaven, there would be no need of 'Christ.' But occultism, although it holds the 'power,' holds neither the 'kingdom' nor the 'glory,' for these are of Christ. The adept knows not the kingdom of heaven, and 'the least in this kingdom are greater than he.'

"'Desire *first* the kingdom of God and God's righteousness; and all these things shall be added unto you.' As Jesus said of Prometheus[89], 'Take no thought for to-morrow. Behold the lilies of the field and the birds of the air, and trust God as these,' For the saint has faith; the adept has knowledge. If the adepts in occultism or in physical science could suffice to man, I would have committed no message to you. But the two are not in opposition. All things are yours, even the kingdom and the power, but the glory is to God. Do not be ignorant of their teaching, for I would have you know all. Take, therefore, every means to know. This knowledge is of man, and cometh from the mind. Go, therefore, to man to learn it. 'If you will be perfect, learn also of these.' 'Yet the wisdom which is from above, is above all.' For one man may begin from within, that is, with wisdom, and wisdom is one with love. Blessed is the man who chooseth wisdom, for she leaveneth all things. And another man may begin from without, and that which is without is power. To such there shall be a thorn in the flesh[90]. For it is hard in such case to attain to the within. But if a man be first wise inwardly, he shall the more easily have this also added unto him. For he is born again and is free. Whereas at a great price must the adept buy freedom. Nevertheless, I bid you seek;—and in this also you shall find. But I have shown you a more excellent way than theirs. Yet both Ishmael and Isaac are sons of one father, and of all her children is Wisdom justified. So neither are they wrong, nor are you led astray. The goal is the same; but their way is harder than yours. They take the kingdom by violence, if they take it, and by much toil and agony of the flesh. But from the time of Christ within you, the kingdom is open to the sons of God. Receive what you can receive; I would have you know all things. And if you have served seven years for wisdom, count it not loss to serve seven years for power also. For if Rachel bear the best beloved, Leah hath many sons, and is exceeding fruitful. But her eye is not single; she looketh two ways, and seeketh not that which is above only. But to you Rachel is given first, and perchance her beauty may suffice. I say not, let it suffice; it is better to know all things, for if you know not all, how can you judge all? For as a man heareth, so must he judge. Will you therefore be regenerate in the without, as well as in the within? For they are renewed in the body, but you in the soul. It is well to be baptised into John's baptism, if a man receive also the Holy Ghost. But some know not so much as that there is any Holy Ghost. Yet Jesus also, being Himself regenerate in the spirit, sought unto the Baptism of John, for thus it became Him to fulfil Himself in all things. And having fulfilled, behold, the 'Dove' descended on Him. If then you will be perfect, seek both that which is within and that which is without; and the circle of being, which is the 'wheel of life,' shall be complete in you."

The Scriptural allusions in this teaching, which was received by "Mary" under illumination occurring in sleep, proved to be on the lines of the Kabala.

There were sundry other tokens of recognition which are entitled to reproduction here, as showing to how wide a range of educated and intelligent opinion within the pale of Christianity our work appeals. Their value is due to their representing a class of minds which, while possessed of the ordinary ecclesiastical training, are not restricted to the knowledge thereby acquired. For, seeing that such training means little, if anything, more than the mechanical learning of what other men have said who, themselves, had no real knowledge, the opinions, expressed on the strength of it, are neither educated nor intelligent, but adoptive only and perfunctory, and represent learning without insight. And as such precisely are the opinions which constitute ecclesiastical orthodoxy, the judgment of the representatives of that orthodoxy on our work possesses no more real value than did that of Caiaphas and his coadjutors on Jesus and His work[91]. Denouncing Him as a blasphemer, they were themselves blasphemers. And inasmuch as they were types of the votaries of ecclesiastical orthodoxy of all time, it is obvious that the only new revelation—if any—which would find acceptance at their hands, would be one that confirmed and reinforced their errors, instead of exposing and correcting them. Proceeding, as was declared by Jesus, from their "father, the devil," a priest-constructed system ever prefers Barabbas to Christ;— prefers, that is, a system which defrauds—hence the force of the term "robber" as applied to Barabbas—man of the divine potentialities which Christ came to reveal to him by demonstrating them in His own person, together with the manner of their realisation.

Not that all who bear the title of Ecclesiastics come under this condemnation. In every age of the Church there have been those who, while holding office in it, have not consented to the "Scarlet Woman" of Sacerdotalism. And never was there a time when the proportion of these was larger, or when their sense of the need of a New Gospel of Interpretation was more keen and urgent than now: so intolerable to multitudes of the clergy of all sections of the Church has become the antagonism recognised by them as subsisting between the traditional and official presentation of religion and their own clear perceptions of goodness and truth[92].

The testimonies which remain to be added are valuable as coming from men who, while possessed of ecclesiastical training, have been taught also of the Spirit, and, adding to tradition intuition, and to learning insight, have in themselves the witness to that which they utter.

A distinguished French ecclesiastic, the Abbé Roca, writing in *L'Aurore*, says of our books—

"These books seem to me to be the chosen organs of the Divine Feminine" (*i.e.* the interpretative) "Principle, in view of the new revelation of Revelation."

By which it will be seen that he shared Cardinal Newman's expectation referred to in the introduction; and accepted as realised the forecast of Joseph de Maistre when he said "Religion and Science, in virtue of their natural affinity, will meet in the brain of some man of genius—perhaps of more than one—and the world will get what it needs and cries for, *not a new religion, but the revelation of Revelation.*" As the event shows, for "the brain of some man," he should have said "the mind and soul of a woman."

The Rev. Dr. John Pulsford, author of "The Supremacy of Man," "Quiet Hours," "Morgenrothe," and other works distinguished for the depth of their piety and insight, thus wrote to me on the publication of "Clothed with the Sun"—

"I cannot tell you with what thankfulness and pleasure I have read *Clothed with the Sun*. It is impossible for a spiritually intelligent reader to doubt that these teachings were received from *within* the astral veil. They are full of the concentrated and compact wisdom of the Holy Heavens and of God. If Christians knew their own religion, they would find in these priceless records our Lord Christ and His vital process abundantly illustrated and confirmed. The regret is that so few, comparatively, who read the book, will be aware of the tithe of its pearls. But that such communications are possible, and are permitted to be given to the world, is a sign, and a most promising sign of our age.

"It is no little joy to me to feel that I am so much more in sympathy with God's daughter, the Seeress, than I supposed. The testimony is so clearly above, and distinct from, aught that is derived from the occult powers of the universe, rather than from the Supreme Spirit and Father-Mother of our Spirits."

Another notable student of spiritual science, a Priest, writing in *Light* of 21st October, 1882, after describing *The Perfect Way* as "that most wonderful of all books which has appeared since the beginning of the Christian Era," said:—"It is a book that no student can be without if he will know *the truth* on these matters. It furnishes us with a master-key to the phenomena which so perplex the minds of enquirers, and gives a system, the like of which has not been seen for eighteen centuries." The late Rev. John Manners, a man venerable of years and mature of spirit, and deeply versed in the sciences of both worlds, declared of these illuminations, "the Great I Am speaks in every line of them. Only the Logos Himself could be their source." Lady Caithness, already referred to, upon receiving a copy of *The Perfect Way*, wrote: "I have got another Bible, the *most complete* Revelation, *certainly*, that has yet been given to man on this planet"[93]. And a Parsee scholar, a native of India, wrote: "*The Perfect Way* has made me a much nobler man—a man of tranquility and calmness, due to the knowledge of the philosophy of Being imbibed by me from it, and for which my mind was fortunately prepared"[94].

As stated in the preface, this present book is intended but as an epitome and instalment of the far larger book in course of preparation. For, as with the old Gospel of Manifestation, so with the New Gospel of Interpretation, the excusable hyperbole is no less appropriate to it,—"I suppose that even the world itself could not contain the books which might be written."

For the human soul is a theme as inexhaustible as it is paramount. And, as never in the world's history have the need and the desire for the knowledge of it been so urgent as they now are, so never in the world's history has there been a revelation of it comparable with that which has been vouchsafed in our day, and is contained in the narrative, the completion of which, and this alone, will enable me to "depart in peace," having no apprehension of after disquietude on the score of having left unaccomplished a portion so important of the task committed to me.

THE END.

Milton Keynes UK
Ingram Content Group UK Ltd.
UKHW031925221024
2303UKWH00004B/292

9 789362 928047